Confessions of a Former Michigan Prosecutor

Attorney Jonathan A. Paul

DEDICATION

To those who are motivated to change the perception of their case

CONTENTS

INTRODUCTION

Prior to entering private practice as a criminal defense lawyer, I spent years as a prosecutor in both New York City and Michigan. When I graduated from the University of Michigan Law School in 2007, I wanted to get immediate experience in the courtroom.

Most graduates of top-ten law schools go off and make the big bucks at major law firms around the country. They sit in back offices working on cases assigned to them by a partner, and once all the grunt work is done, it's handed off to the partner to get praise and get paid by the client.

If you work thousands of hours a year, abandon your family for long enough and produce a good enough work product for 8-10 years, then you get to play partner and hand off work to young lawyers. This seemed like a death sentence to me, and I was not interested in being paid to sit in a dark room and be a paper pusher who got zero credit other than a nice paycheck. Was that really what being a lawyer is all about?

I grew up in New York City and watched Law & Order on a regular basis. My idea of being a lawyer was Jack McCoy prosecuting the big cases, and always winning in the end. There would be ups and down, but hard work, persistence and the truth would prevail.

I never thought I would be a lifer as a prosecutor, but I recognized the unique hands on, front lines experience offered by the position. In New York City, there are literally millions of criminal cases charged each year, and well someone has to work on them. Due to case volume, you get a lot of responsibility and not a ton of oversight or help on day one - it's sink or swim.

I worked at the Brooklyn DA's Office on Jay Street in Downtown Brooklyn where we had over a thousand prosecutors; we weren't paid like most lawyers at the big firms, but we were paid in patience, experience and opportunity.

We were handed 100's of files each day, told to go to a courtroom and deal with 20-30 experienced criminal lawyers trying to trick you, and push you in the direction they wanted the case to go. The judge didn't care that you had no idea what you were doing. The phone would be ringing all day about my other cases in different courtrooms while I was trying to focus on what the other lawyers and judge were trying to tell me in my courtroom. It was stressful, I made mistakes, and I was worked hard with little financial reward, but I was getting better each day.

I spent late nights in the Early Case Assessment Bureau (ECAB), working with detectives on extremely serious and emotional cases that JUST happened. Literally speaking to a rape victim within hours of the horror she endured. Going to the hospital to speak to victims who were brutally attacked and injured to get statements. I was on call to go out to scenes of crimes in the middle of the night, and expected to be the law enforcement leader and prosecutor among police officers, detectives and other emergency responders. I would then wake up early and be in court on those 100's of files, expected to be prepared for multiple trials and hearings each day.

I eventually moved to Michigan with my wife, but my work as a prosecutor was not yet done. I decided to join the Oakland

County Prosecutor's Office, which was the New York City version of the Manhattan DA's Office. The Brooklyn DA's Office was very much like working in Detroit for Wayne County, but Oakland County was like Manhattan - more resources, more prestige and a different working environment.

I no longer had 100's of cases each day in court, and I was not up late into the night talking to victims of serious crimes, because we had enough resources to spread things out as an office. While I was no longer buried in files and 15 hour days, I now had one thing I never had in my past job; I had the resources and time to work on my craft. I could sit down and really learn, and prepare for hearings and trials. I was able to become a better lawyer by having more time to sharpen my litigation skills.

I came to this second job with a lot of confidence, because I had survived and endured my time as a Brooklyn prosecutor. New York City: If You Can Make it Here, You Can Make it Anywhere very much applied to being a prosecutor in Michigan.

In Michigan, I took many cases to trial, both jury and bench, held high level preliminary examinations on serious felonies, did a ton of motions, hearings and worked on 1000's of unique criminal cases. I was learning a new set of laws, rules and procedure coming to Michigan, but actually got to study and learn my trade.

After spending time as a prosecutor in Michigan, I knew it was time to make a move. I never wanted to be a lifer as a prosecutor, because it was not in my personality to prosecute people all of my life. People who commit crimes deserve to be punished, but as a prosecutor you never really learn the backstory or the source of the offense. As a prosecutor you just see a name, a charge and assume "oh that's a criminal, I must prosecute and do my job".

I was also NOT impressed with most criminal attorneys in Michigan - they were simply acting like the opposite of a prosecutor, which seems like it's the role to play, but it's not. As a prosecutor you have a law to prosecute on and facts to use to accomplish that task - little emotion gets in the way of the job. Most defense lawyers believe their role is to simply resist and fight those facts as if they are made up or wrong without humanizing the case. If the criminal lawyer isn't going to humanize the defendant, then who is going to do that? Nobody.

Having played both roles, I can comfortably say 99 percent of people who are charged are at least a little bit guilty. Maybe a prosecutor can't meet their burden and there is not enough evidence to convict on, or there is a technicality to prevent prosecution, but the facts and charges are not made up or completely wrong. Defense lawyers don't quite understand that it's OK to have a guilty client, and it's ok to try to work with the prosecutor to a compromise for both sides. Does a criminal lawyer really want to pat a drunk driver on the back and say "hey no harm no foul, you're fine, go back out there and act the same??" I don't - I would rather help that person as a first priority. This is just common sense lawyering with the big picture in mind.

Based on my experience as a prosecutor, I decided I wanted to be a different kind of criminal defense lawyer. I had a few goals and six principles to go by:

1. I wanted to work with good people, not "criminals" who commit crimes to hurt people, property or are just evil spirited. I don't work on cases that I am not comfortable with. I don't just assume all people are innocent, so if I am not comfortable with the allegations, I won't take on the case - Michigan has 1000's of lawyers to help this person. I want clients who I believe in and can help.

2. I wanted to actually help my client with whatever brought them to my office; this didn't mean "getting them off" but rather to actually work on the reason why they found themselves charged with a crime. If we can get the case dismissed or win a trial, then that's great, but it's more important to help the client with what lead to the allegations in the first place.

3. Wanted motivated clients who were willing to work hard to change the perception of their case from day one. They might be really guilty, and that was ok. It did not make them a bad person, or someone I wouldn't trust in my own life. People make poor choices, it doesn't make them evil people who can't be trusted going forward.

4. Wanted to use this motivation and proactive work product of my client to work with the prosecutor and judge to create better results than people who just come to court looking to fight the charges just to fight the charges because they are not happy with the options. Lawyers don't have time machines or easy buttons. If you broke the law, you can't change the past, but you control the present and your future.

5. Wanted to leverage my client's out of court performance

along with finding enough leverage within the evidence of the case to meet my client's goals without the risk of trial. You need inside and outside leverage to get the best result.

6. Wanted to go to trial on the right cases. Ultimately the client always has the option for trial, but I don't recommend going to trial on a losing case - usually a guilty person with strong evidence against them. If you're innocent then let's go to trial - if you're guilty and the evidence supports it, let's meet your goals in a different way. I don't want to set my client up for failure.

As a criminal defense lawyer, I am very selective in the cases and clients that I take on. Our firm ends up turning down more cases than we take on. Each case and client needs a customized approach, and we develop goals for each case.

My goal for every case is to get to the right result. I want to know my clients goals and put a plan in place to hit every goal. We're aware of the prosecutor and judge and their goals for each case, and we work together to come to the right result.

Some clients go to trial, most work toward resolution, which is hopefully more favorable to the client than it would have been without working with me. This might mean reduction or dismissal of charges, a better more manageable sentence, but most importantly the tools and mindset to go forward a productive and more responsible person for their family, career and life.

RETAIL FRAUD

If you're charged with retail fraud in Michigan, the prosecutor doesn't trust you. The allegation is you stole something from a store, and the prosecutor will assume you were finally caught after years of stealing from multiple stores.

This may or may not be true, but it really doesn't matter, because there is no way to show this isn't the truth; perception runs wild, because the prosecutor can't imagine stealing in their own life as they've kept a straight arrow lifestyle to go on to prosecute cases for a living. This is a crime of fraud, theft and dishonesty and it puts you in a negative light to the government.

Prosecutors also assume these cases are pretty cut and dry; the police report says that loss prevention officer #1 observed the defendant doing X, Y and Z, and hey there's even a video of the incident. Maybe the defendant even admitted to stealing when they were caught. Wow this is an easy case, why wouldn't the defendant just run to the courthouse and plead guilty.

A young prosecutor may not be thinking outside the box and realize that loss prevention officers go on vacation, get fired, relocate, quit their jobs. There may be strong evidence of the crime, but if the witness isn't around, then they have no case.

As a defense attorney, we acknowledge the perception of our audience; we acknowledge that the prosecutor believes they have a strong case and there may be no room for negotiations on the legal issue. We do our due diligence with the evidence, but we focus on creating leverage outside of the courtroom by being proactive. It's likely that the client is very guilty, and well that's OK. I don't need an innocent client as a defense lawyer to win the case.

We need to show that this can be a valuable learning experience for my client; we need to figure out why they stole. We can't throw our hands up in the air and say "we don't know" because that's unpredictable and dangerous to toss my client back into society, unaware why they break the law, because nothing has been done to stop it from happening again. We identify the issue, and work on it. We don't run from it, we embrace the opportunity to be a better person going forward.

We can't go back and change the past, but we control the present, and can project the future for the prosecutor and the judge. We tailor 3-4 proactive steps for the client that allow them to show the other side of them; it is not fair to be judged based upon a single police report. It's only one small factor that goes into understanding my client.

We work with clients from all backgrounds that are charged with retail fraud cases. We tend to get a lot of nurses, educators, neglected spouses and other hard working people who at times feel underappreciated for all of their hard work. Some of these professionals aren't paid what they deserve, and part of that mental state plays a role in how the client finds themselves charged with shoplifting.

Many of our clients are having issues with family, health or working under a lot of stress at the workplace. Along with the aforementioned clients, we've worked with retail fraud clients who work for the IRS as tax agents and work as medical doctors who steal baseball cards from Target. Nothing shocks us anymore when it comes to new clients charged with shoplifting.

If the prosecutor and judge get to know my client while working the proactive program, they see the total person, and are more likely to go along with our course of action for the case. A difficult charge for sure, but a very manageable outcome is likely if the client is ready to work.

DOMESTIC VIOLENCE

As a former prosecutor, I worked on hundreds of domestic violence cases. I've taken that experience, and now help clients accused of this serious crime as a defense attorney.

The first thing we need to do is understand and acknowledge the perception of our audience. This includes the prosecutor, judge, police and the general public. I include the general public, because domestic violence cases go to trial more than most criminal charges, and having a jury of your peers decide your case comes with many pros and cons.

I don't condone violence against family members or loved ones. I take on these types of cases, because despite a serious criminal charge, the accused deserves to execute their rights in the criminal justice system. If the client is falsely accused then I help them push for their innocence; if the client broke the law and the evidence supports the charge, then we focus on getting the client the help they need to be a better person, avoid future violence and make amends to the person hurt by their actions.

I tell clients all the time, it's ok if you're guilty, it doesn't make you a bad person, it doesn't mean you're going to jail, and it may not even mean having a criminal record from the incident. It's an opportunity to work on yourself, be proactive, and change the reality of who you are along with the perception of the case.

In Michigan, a regular assault becomes a domestic assault when it involves a spouse, a former spouse, a person which you share a child in common, a resident or former resident of your household or a person which you have or had a dating relationship.

Because of this close bond relationship, which is required, the prosecutor does not give the accused the benefit of the doubt. Anytime I speak to a prosecutor about a domestic violence charge, there's a major stink in the air. Simply by reading a 1-2 page police report, the prosecutor is convinced my client is really guilty and is ready to plead and beg for mercy from the judge. Prosecutor's, especially less experienced ones, don't bother to see both sides of the case; the majority of domestic violence cases begin with a mutual dispute, and typically two parties are at fault in the incident starting, and usually in the police getting involved.

Once the incident has started, does one party break the law with a violent act, or does one person just get arrested based on who placed the call. Does the male get arrested simply due to public perception? Are their real and actual injuries (although not required) that can help us better understand the case?

There's unlikely to be a video unless it happens in public, but photos taken of the parties involved, medical reports, audio from 911 calls, officer microphones while on scene and dash cam videos can be helpful.

The rules of evidence for domestic violence cases provide the prosecutor additional ammo to admit certain evidence against a client if the victim/witness testifies to something different at trial than originally stated to law enforcement.

As a former prosecutor, I can see the wheels spinning in their head; sure the report looks strong, but are you able to actually put this forth at trial and meet your burden? Maybe not. My clients always keep a trial on the table for domestic violence cases, because unlike most cases, a private citizen is the key witness, not a police officer, and there's probably not going to be videos, tests etc like say a drunk driving case.

My clients must use this elephant in the room to their advantage. These cases usually start with people who love each other, get involved in an incident, but within 24 hours are back loving each other. Is the prosecution willing to force someone to testify if their story has changed? Are they going to issue a material witness warrant and arrest someone to testify?

Along with this leverage, my clients have to create leverage outside of the courtroom. We understand the perception of my client. and the uncertainly that the charges bring for my client in the mind of the prosecutor and judge.

Is my client a dangerous person? Should they be locked up? Should they have to avoid the person and the place where this happened?

No matter what the actual answer to those questions are, we lean toward acknowledging that these are not worth fighting over at the moment, we simply get to work to show they aren't true.

If alcohol was involved, I get my clients on a daily testing unit to show that they are clearheaded during the case, and if alcohol was a major contributor to the incident, we put a lot of our focus on substance abuse awareness and treatment. If the evidence indicates there actually was some form of violence, we may engage in proactive anger management and/or counseling. If based on the evidence, it appears that resolution may be the best route, we may even begin an actual domestic violence program.

If the parties wish to have contact, I am able to make contact with the alleged victim/witness to inform them that if they wish to provide additional information about wanting contact with my client, they can come to the next court hearing. A judge may or may not grant this request now, but my client needs the victim to agree for this to happen. If things are still red hot, I tell my client they are better off not having contact right now; the worse thing to happen is for my client to have contact, and another argument breaks out, and the cops are back at the scene. That's a potential bond violation and new charges.

Each case is different, but the perception of the prosecution rarely changes for domestic violence. This is always a hot button issue for a prosecutor, which it should be, but the prosecutor has to be asked to keep an open mind and the defense must be able to play some currency when it comes to discussing positive outcomes for the client. It's quite difficult to sway a prosecutor on simply statements like: he has no record, he has a job, kids etc. This is not a low level everyday OPPS my client made a mistake. Domestic violence charges must be met with a serious response; mere allegations are enough for my client to get to work on changing the perception of the case.

MISDEMEANOR ASSAULT

As a former prosecutor, I always viewed cases within categories in terms of hot button and cool button topics. While all crimes are considered serious enough to prosecute, there is a difference between driving with a suspended license and assaulting someone. The deciding factor in determining hot vs cool button issue was "was someone hurt or almost hurt" by this offense.

If another person was a victim, the prosecutor must consider their feelings and opinion and can't quite make quick deals in a vacuum to resolve cases. If that person was injured emotionally or physically then you're dealing with potential medical issues, restitution etc. An assault case in Michigan falls under this hot button issue for a prosecutor. Easy, quick deals can't be made when others are involved in the case. Victims can hold up deals and apply pressure on the prosecution to push the case to trial if necessary with no offers other than a plea as charged.

When I represent a client charged with assault, it's important to understand the identity of the alleged victim; do they know my client? Is there a history between the parties? Next, are there any witnesses, video or evidence other than the statements of the client and the victim. This outside evidence could sway a case one way or another, no matter the statements of the parties involved.

Next, although my client is charged, I need to determine if there is an argument for self-defense or mutual combatant where both parties should either be charged or not charged. Is it really fair to just pick one person to call the victim and one person to call the defendant? It happens a lot in Michigan. Assault cases are not easy cases for a prosecutor if held to the proper burden of guilty beyond a reasonable doubt, especially with a he/she vs he/she conflicting stories. The tie goes to not guilty if a jury can't decide who to believe. If we can find enough of an argument during the pretrial phase, we can sway the prosecution to view the case as "well both parties are at fault here", and reasonable minds can resolve the case.

Along with exploring the strengths and weaknesses in the case itself, my client is creating leverage outside of the courtroom. If alcohol was involved, we're focusing on substance abuse treatment and or awareness along with voluntary daily alcohol testing.

We may be engaged in counseling and community service among other proactive steps, because we're doing what's within our power to help the case every single day. Will we need these steps if the case is dismissed, or we win at trial? No, but what if the case isn't heading the way we expected, and we need a backup plan? What if the jury or judge despite the truth, find my client guilty, there's no do overs.

My clients acknowledge the perception of their audience and say, no matter the outcome of this case, I find myself in this vulnerable position; I can't go back in time and change the evidence, but I can control the present perception of who I am and determine my own future. Common goals for assault cases are to avoid jail, avoid a criminal conviction, receive a manageable outcome that allows for travel, continuation of career, and to live a healthy, productive and hopefully a more fulfilling and informed lifestyle.

FELONY ASSAULT

In Michigan, a simple assault becomes a felonious assault when a dangerous weapon is involved. This could be your typical idea of a weapon (knife, bat, brass knuckles) or something less obvious like a lamp, toaster or a high heel.

The term "assault" means that you placed someone in immediate fear of a battery. Therefore, simply pointing a knife at someone, if it that makes them think that they may be stabbed or injured is the definition of a felonious assault in Michigan.

As a former prosecutor who handled many felony assault cases, the two things I would look for would be the "weapon" used and if their were any injuries. Someone swinging a knife around at least to me was more serious in nature than someone throwing a toaster oven at another person. Both could hurt someone, and both are serious crimes, but I tried to examine the mindset of the defendant. In my mind at least, you pull a knife to hurt someone or scare them, the very definition of assault; you probably throw a toaster in the heat of the moment rather than an intention to hurt someone.

I would then look at what happened with that weapon. There is a more serious charge in Michigan called Assault with Intent to Commit Bodily Harm Less than Murder that could be charged, and likely if the person used a knife and actually hurt the person.

A knife stabbing is more likely to do great bodily harm than throwing the toaster oven at someone. But, that toaster oven, could either hit the wall and not the victim or bruise/injure the victim pretty good. That difference could mean different outcomes at least from what the prosecutor would offer in your typical case.

If the defendant lacked a violent criminal history, and the case would have been a misdemeanor assault, but for a funky fact like a toaster or a lamp were involved as a "dangerous weapon", I would be more likely to be open to dismissing a felony and potentially reducing to a misdemeanor, or having an open mind to a first offender type program. While this might be my mindset, I want to know a lot more about the person charged.

As a criminal defense attorney, I rely on that knowledge and know that if the prosecutor is willing to keep an open mind, I still need to justify that decision for the prosecutor. If alcohol was involved in the incident, we're alcohol testing voluntarily on day one. We're engaged in community service work, potentially in counseling, maybe taking anger management classes. If the charges stem from domestic violence, and both parties are agreeable and the contact is allowed, we might do some couples counseling.

We must go above and beyond and show the key players (prosecutor and judge) that your typical Saturday night is NOT using a deadly weapon against friends, family and neighbors. We try to better understand how we got to this point, and work on the trigger/driving force. It might be alcohol, might be a hostile relationship with the victim, general anger management/self-control issues. Better for us to identify the issue, and work on it then the judge and prosecutor to judge you based on a single moment in time; a felony with a deadly weapon.

MISDEMEANOR DRUG POSSESSION

As a former prosecutor, I handled hundreds of possession of marijuana cases. For purposes of this posting, we are only discussing misdemeanor possession, which is a one year misdemeanor in Michigan. There are other more serious marijuana offenses in Michigan, which involve sale, manufacturing and large quantities.

For example a sale of marijuana in Michigan up to, but less than 5kg is a 5-year felony, 5 to 45kg is a 7-year felony and 45kg or more is a 15-year felony.

This also excludes cases that relate to individuals who have a valid medical marijuana card, but are still charged with marijuana related charges due to some alleged non-compliance with the medical marijuana law.

As a prosecutor, I personally viewed marijuana cases in two different ways, and the main differing factor was prior criminal history. If the person had a clear criminal history then there were many avenues to resolving these type of cases with the defense attorney in the case, such as the Holmes Youthful Trainee Act or MCL 333.7411. If the person charged did not qualify for one of these programs then options were more limited for resolution.

To my surprise many people just wanted to plead guilty and move on from the case; many judges would be just fine the person and move on from the case, which was surprising as well. While it was not my business as the prosecutor, I always shook my head in disbelief that someone would stick themselves with a criminal drug record just to move on from a problem. This was such a short-term mindset, and when I say short, I mean once they hit the parking lot their entire life was changed as a convicted drug criminal.

for the cases where clients were eligible, the Trainee Act (HYTA) applies to parties charged within a certain age bracket and the "7411" relates to lack of prior drug offenses. If one of these options was available to the person charged, these cases were typically resolved. As a prosecutor these cases seemed pretty simple, but once I went to the defense side, I realized how much more work and effort should be put into these type of cases to get the client the very best result.

As a criminal defense attorney in Michigan, I have to anticipate that even when a case is resolved in a favorable way, that the case is not over for the client. Any dismissal type program in Michigan does require a term of probation, and if the original charge is drug related, well my client will be drug testing during probation. It's not shocking that someone who used and possessed marijuana in the past, may use again even though the stakes are high on probation. A client who violates probation can have the dismissal deal taken away and they can go to jail.

Not only does the person then have a criminal record, but a driver's license can be suspended if the charge is reported to the Michigan Secretary of State.

My goal in representing a client charged with possession of marijuana in Michigan is three-fold.

1 - Get them the very best outcome on their case, which is typically some sort of dismissal program unless there is an issue with the search or testing of the substance, which we might file

a motion or go to trial. Each case and client is different, and those options are discussed with each client.

2 - Set them up for success if they are on probation, which means limiting requirements, tasks, time frame and closing as many loopholes as possible.

3 - Set the person up for success long-term. If they were self-medicating and have a medical need for the marijuana, but didn't have a card at the time, I encourage them to attempt to make their possession and use legal once the case is over. There are actually some judges that allow a valid medical marijuana card holder to use the substance while on probation.

For #1, a straight plea to possession of marijuana is the most common outcome with one of the dismissal programs. These dismissal outcomes need to be in-line with the prosecutor and judge; even if someone is eligible, it does not mean it's guaranteed; a judge must agree, and depending on your case, a prosecutor may have to agree as well for one of the program. Prior dismissals are counted against you and could limit your ability to be approved for both programs. Some judges and prosecutors are just "tough" and don't just agree, they need to be convinced, and that's now always easy.

Ideally, I am able to turn possession into use of marijuana for a client along with the dismissal deal. I call that the "double dismissal". Possible with some prosecutors and judges, but not most.

Although it's our goal that nothing goes on one's record, we need to plan for worst case scenarios. Lowering the charge on day one could mean avoiding a license suspension, and the maximum jail sentence is 90 days, and not one year. We may also be able to turn possession into a drug paraphernalia charge, which is also a 90 day misdemeanor. Better to get the dismissal on two fronts.

For #2, there's a big difference between 24 months of probation and 6 months of probation. Probation is both length and requirements. When I take on a possession of marijuana case my clients are proactive from day one, which means drug testing, education and or treatment, volunteer work, potential counseling etc. We get a head start in the process and create a safety net. I've had cases that would typically carry a 12 to 24 month probation sentences, instead carry end of probation review days within weeks of sentencing rather than months and years. My clients can't change the past, because we don't have a time machine, but we do control the present and can impact your future.

For #3, as I stated above, if the client truly needs marijuana for a medical reason, and can have a doctor agree, then they should go ahead and pursue the medical marijuana license. The court is only in your business for a short period of time, and that period can be quite short if you do everything you can upfront to change the perception of your case. Setting a client up for long-term success means making better choices, identifying the consequences of your decisions both in the short and long-term, and avoiding future pitfalls.

FELONY DRUG POSSESSION

As a former prosecutor in Michigan and New York City, my colleagues viewed drug cases within different categories. It's one thing if the person charged is simply a drug addict who possesses the drugs for personal use. There are many programs within the prosecutor's office and the local courts to get this person the help they need to get off the drug and back to a normal and productive life. There is also a door open to work toward resolution to avoid jail and potentially a criminal record.

Most prosecutors and judges are willing to give this type of a person a second chance in life if they are willing to earn the result. Programs that depend on your age, but also a program that doesn't have any age requirement to receive the possibility of a dismissal upon successful completion of probation.

It's another thing if this person is possessing the drugs, and there are indicators that they may be selling the drugs to the public. This opens up the door for additional charges, and there is less tolerance and patience for someone who is contributing to the drug epidemic. These type of offenses are typically not eligible for first offender type programs, and jail is more likely for a case of this nature.

As a defense attorney, the great majority of my felony drug possession cases have been the first type of person. Someone who possesses the drugs for personal use. Occasionally the client is a teenager or young adult who may be possessing the drugs to both consume and share with friends. Although this trickles a bit into that more serious category, there is some understanding/tolerance if the client is on the younger end of the spectrum, and can take the case as a valuable life lesson and earn an exceptional outcome, rather than be branded a felon for the rest of their life for a poor choice as a young adult.

Let's assume I am working with a 20 year old college student. The client is doing well in school, has no prior criminal history, but the police arrest the client for possessing heroin, cocaine or another felony level substance. First off, there is no legal reason to possess this type of drug; this is no medical purpose like there is for medical marijuana in Michigan. Assuming any stop and search was done within the law, my client is caught red handed. As long as the substance comes back as a felony controlled substance, there isn't much wiggle room.

If the substance is a prescription drug like Alprazolam, Xanax, opiates or another common drug, and my client does not have a valid prescription, they don't have a defense to possessing the drug. If the client had a prior prescription and can show that, it may provide us a bit of context into the current possession, but it's not a true defense. Pills in Michigan are referred to as analogues under the law.

My client and I have to acknowledge the perception of our audience, and begin to change the perception of the case. The most important thing to do is to STOP using the substance and SHOW YOUR WORK. That means we begin proactive drug testing right away. Felony drug cases are not charged immediately, because the substance must be tested at a lab; this could take weeks or months. The worst thing to do is just let time go by without SHOWING YOUR WORK. It's a nice first line to inform the arraigning judge down the road that your client has been voluntarily testing and passed all tests since this incident.

Next, we need to consider why the client was in possession of the substance. Are we dealing with a true addiction where we need intensive treatment, or is this a client trying to be cool among his/her friends and using it for recreational purposes. If it's the second, we might want to focus more on the positive life adjustments and working on appreciating risk and decision making in their young minds.

The key is to identify WHY the client was in possession and do our best to eliminate the reason for possessing it so it doesn't happen again going forward. Addicts need treatment, risk takers need to increase their insight and awareness about making better long-term choices in life, and reflect back upon their decisions and how they fit into the context of the long term viability as productive members of society.

As a defense attorney, if I can show a prosecutor and judge that my client has not used the substance over a period of time since the incident, and we've identified the WHY for possession and we're working on a solution, there is a greater chance that doors will open for a favorable resolution for my client.

DRIVING WHILE LICENSE SUSPENDED

As a former prosecutor, I worked on many suspended license cases. While this is a criminal misdemeanor, it certainly fell toward the bottom of priority cases as a prosecutor. The most important thing I would look for when working on this type of case, is why is the license suspended, and what was the person doing at the time they came into contact with the police?

If their license is suspended because of a drunk driving charge and they are in violation of that suspension then there will less leeway to have sympathy for the defendant. If you plead to drunk driving or are found guilty at trial, you serve your suspension as the law dictates; there's a good reason why you're not driving. If your license is suspended, because you owe money to the Secretary of State because of past due traffic tickets or driver responsibility fees, I personally viewed these cases with a lot more empathy for the defendant.

The Michigan Secretary of State is greedy, and are well known for racking up late fees, extra fees and creating a lot of red tape for drivers. With this mind, I was always open to trying to work with the person charged; if they needed some time to clear up money owed, I would give a 30-60 day adjournment to allow some time to clean things up. I did not want to stick them with a DWLS charge and make things worse for their situation. If things were cleaned up, I would usually offer a non-DWLS type offense such as No Operators License on Person or another non-abstractable offense. Sometimes it was nearly impossible for the person to clean things up due to finances, and those situations would be taken on a case by case basis for reductions.

The case by case process usually came down to what the person was doing when driving. Was it 1 pm on a Saturday with a no right turn on red violation while driving their child to the urgent care or the emergency room, or was it 1 am and they were speeding at 90 miles per hour in a 55 mph zone. I'm going to give that first person a break, especially if they can show me documentation of the medical issue.

As a criminal defense lawyer in Michigan who helps clients charged with DWLS, I do the same thing I did as a prosecutor. I run my client's driving record to better understand the nature of the suspension, and anticipate how the prosecutor may view my client's case. I also get as much information about the incident as possible to understand why my client came in contact with the police, and the circumstances surrounding the police contact. I try to better understand why my client decided to drive against the law. Were they even aware of the suspension? Is the wrong address on file?

Might we have a rare case where my client's operation is in question? If the officer only shows up on the scene when the car is no longer in motion, is it a slam dunk my client was driving?

We create as much leverage as we can around the circumstances and facts of the case, but we're also shaping the perception of the client for the prosecutor and judge. When my client walks into court, the few things the prosecutor and judge know about about them are their name, the criminal charge of driving on a suspended license, why the license was suspended and why the cops came in contact with my client. None of this is going to be positive for my client.

As their attorney, I acknowledge the viewpoint of the other side, but look to add to that package of information. Providing more information on my client's family, career, background etc. We also add elements such as a driver improvement course, some community service; if there's any mental or emotional issues, we may even get a counselor involved. This may seem like "too much" for having a suspended license, but why not? It only helps improve the perception of who you are if you're willing to put in the extra work and show who you are outside of this incident. If you want an extraordinary result, you need to go above and beyond.

My number one goal for a DWLS type case is to push for a dismissal of the original charge. We want something that is not going to impact your driving record, and we ideally want to avoid probation, and potentially walk away with credit for the proactive items we completed and pay a small fine.

PROBATION VIOLATION

The most common sentence for a defendant in Michigan is a term of probation. For a misdemeanor, a defendant can receive up to 24 months, and for a felony it can be 60 months. There is reporting probation and non-reporting, and there are standard conditions of probation such as no alcohol, drugs, no new offenses, keep the probation officer updated on address changes, seek permission to leave the state among other conditions etc.

All probation staffs are different; testing, requirements, meetings will vary by courthouse. Some probation officers will be more flexible with technical violations and allow the person to cure the issue, and not immediately issue a violation to the judge for a Show Cause hearing. Let's assume for the purposes of this writing that the defendant has violated probation, and the probation officer has submitted a violation; the court has set the matter for a Show Cause hearing or an immediate violation of probation hearing.

As a former prosecutor, I was not updated on these violations. If the violations popped up on the docket, I would be dealing with limited information. As a prosecutor, the safest bet is always to argue against the defendant and his/her lawyer and try to uphold some false sense of justice that breaking a rule means someone should be punished. This certainly applies if its a misdemeanor violation and you're dealing with a young prosecutor.

When a prosecutor doesn't know what to say, they surely aren't going to support the defendant's position or take on the case, but rather argue against it as a true opponent. I did the same when I was caught off guard by a judge who wanted to know what my position.

As a criminal defense attorney who helps clients with violations of probation, I apply my past experience and make sure that I speak to the prosecutor beforehand and give them a heads up about the violation. If they were taken by surprise, I fully expect them to argue against me even if they don't really believe it or care.

If I represent a client in a probation violation, it's a two-step process:

1. We come to court with something new. I don't let my client simply show on a VOP (violation of probation) and beg a judge to go easy on them; that's not doing my job, but that's what most other attorneys do. If it's an alcohol violation or a drug violation, well I am already getting my client on more frequent testing; if it's alcohol we are probably on a portable daily device already. Up the AA meetings, jump into counseling etc.

I punch my client right in the gut and "punish" them before the judge has a chance to do it. A client can handle my punch, but may not be able to handle going to jail, losing out on a great deal worked out on their case. You can lose HYTA, 7411, 771.1, MIP first offender, 769.4A type programs for violating your probation.

When we walk into court we can take a lot of wind out of the judge's sails by saying we're already taking steps to address the violation. Sure the judge may still put on a show, but what are they going to say? You shouldn't have stepped up in a big way to address it yourself?

We can usually pause, reflect and buy some time. If we can get a judge to back off taking action, that's a big win. If my client still has months to go on probation, why not accept what we've done already and see how the client does on the "new" plan; you always need a shiny new toy when you go see the judge.

It really depends on the original charge and the violation, but there's a major opportunity to turn a losing hand into a survival situation where you're back on your feet.

2. The second part of the plan is to talk to the prosecutor before the case is called and provide them information about the violation and the steps above. I was a very laid back and amenable prosecutor, but if I was caught off guard I was going to take the easier/less risky route of just piling on the defendant and appearing to be disappointed about the violation and "seeking further justice" and "punishment" because most prosecutors just assume all defendants are "criminals”

If you explain to the prosecutor what's going on, show them the steps you've taken to address the violation, it's very possible to turn them into a neutral party rather than an opponent. It's even possible to have the prosecutor back your steps and tell the judge the same.

If both the defendant and prosecutor both want the judge to put their sword down, delay a decision, back off, the judge is more likely to buy into the plan. It's so important to try to build consensus with the prosecutor. Great to say "your honor, the prosecutor and myself had a very positive conversation on this matter, and it sounds like they are open to X or in agreement with X.

BOND VIOLATION

As a former prosecutor, I was usually not aware of a bond violation when I went to the courthouse with a stack of cases. I would go to court prepared to discuss the case with the defense, but was not updated on bond violations. I would be surprised when a case was called and the judge started grilling the defendant about a violation. The judge would then turn to me as a prosecutor and ask what I thought about the violation.

As a young prosecutor, I would usually take the opposite opinion of whatever the defense lawyer was saying as if I really had a stake in the case. Sure, as a prosecutor it's our job to prosecute and uphold the law, but if the defendant is violating his bond, is it REALLY our business? It has nothing to do with the original incident or the outcome of the case.

Looking back I was probably too harsh on defendant's without knowing the full story. A positive alcohol test, drug test, failing to show up for a court requirement; most of the time the defendant probably did technically violate, but I failed to really think beyond the allegation itself, and the other side of the case.

Things were different if the defense attorney talked to me beforehand and tried to build consensus with me. If I was aware of the issue , I would be more neutral if I had some time to think about it and hear out the other side, but being in the dark and prompted to respond, it was just easier to GO HARD after the defendant and play the anti-defense role. In a way it's how prosecutors are trained.

Based on that experience as a prosecutor, I handle these bond violations much differently than other attorneys I have worked with in my past role. My plan is two-fold for a bond violation in Michigan:

1. We come to court with something new. I don't let my client simply show on a bond violation and beg a judge to go easy on them; that's not doing my job, but that's what most other attorneys do. Many lawyers think that a client's words become magical if they come from an attorney's mouth; that's such a lazy approach. Your client is relying on you to have a plan, so have a plan!

If it's an alcohol violation or a drug violation, well I am already getting my client on more frequent testing; if it's alcohol we are probably on a portable daily device already. Up the AA, jump into counseling, do an Impact Weekend, heck maybe you need to check into rehab. What's a judge going to do, grab you out of inpatient treatment, and send you to jail? Very unlikely!

I punch my client right in the gut and "punish" them before the judge has a chance to do it. A client can handle my punch, but may not be able to handle going to jail, losing out on a dismissal deal offered, because the judge will no longer accept it.

When we walk into court we can take a lot of wind out of the judge's fury by showing that we're already taking steps to address the violation. Sure the judge may still put on a show and act disappointed or angry, but we can't change what happened, why are we wasting our time focusing on that? Well if you don't bring anything new to the table you're only going to be talking about past events. What's the judge going to say if put new items into place?

You shouldn't have stepped up in a big way to address it yourself? No way.

We can usually pause, reflect and buy some time. We may be able to push a potential violation off until the end of the case and "see how the client does". It really depends on the original charge and the violation, but there's a major opportunity to turn a losing hand into a survival situation where you're back on your feet.

I've done this many times. Example being the following:

Let's say the client is charged with assault. They are arraigned and told to refrain from the use of alcohol. Between the arraignment and pretrial my client is randomly tested for alcohol and blows positive. For most cases, the client is in big trouble here; not only do they have a serious charge, now they violated a court order. A judge can revoke bond and stick them in jail, and it might sour the negotiations with the prosecutor if the client is already screwing up.

I would immediately turn the case into not only an assault case, but an alcohol case. My client would jump into an alcohol assessment and evaluation, jump into AA meetings and go on a daily testing device. Over the top? Maybe, but what's the alternative, spending a weekend or more in jail and losing out on a potential great deal? If you screw up, take ownership and do something about it, don't just beg the judge to look the other way or apologize. That's how people ruin their future by screwing up and not taking on the responsibility of their decisions. You are already in court for something negative, don't make it worse. If you're drinking on bond against a court order, we have things to work on. By putting these items into place, a judge is likely to adjourn the bond violation until the conclusion of the case and could essentially do a "time served" on the violation if he/she sees clean tests for 30-60 days etc. Punish yourself and a judge doesn't need to do it.

2. The second part of the plan is to talk to the prosecutor before the case is called and provide them information about the violation and the steps above. I was a very laid back and amenable prosecutor, but if I was caught off guard I was going to take the easier/less risky route of just piling on the defendant and appearing to be disappointed about the violation and "seeking further justice" and "punishment" because most prosecutors just assume all defendants are "criminals" and can't be trusted.

If you explain to the prosecutor what's going on, show them the steps you've taken to address the violation, it's very possible to turn them into a neutral party rather than an opponent. It's even possible to have the prosecutor back your steps and tell the judge the same.

If both the defendant and prosecutor both want the judge to put their sword down, delay a decision, back off, the judge is more likely to buy into the plan. It's so important to try to build consensus with the prosecutor. Great to say "your honor, the prosecutor and myself had a very positive conversation on this matter, and it sounds like they are open to X or in agreement with X. If the prosecutor isn't seeking anything and they are in agreement with our path, things are going to be a lot easier to navigate with the judge.

RECKLESS & CARELESS DRIVING

As a former prosecutor, I worked on many Reckless and Careless Driving cases. The great majority of these cases were based on a ticket issued by a police officer, and rarely had a police report, statements or other evidence. Occasionally we may have had a video from the police cruiser or a private video recording from a residence or commercial property. There's a major difference between these two type of charges.

In Michigan, Reckless Driving is a criminal misdemeanor punishable by 93 days in jail. It can also suspend your driver's license for 90 days and put six points on your driving record. This means potential increases in car insurance and depending on your driving record, it could trigger additional license sanctions.

In contrast, Careless Driving is a civil infraction, which is not punishable by jail time, and does not alone suspend your license, but rather adds three points to your driving record.

Let's start with the Reckless Driving. As a former prosecutor I typically only had a ticket with a charge on it; the lack of a police report put me in a tough situation to evaluate the case; I had to rely upon talking directly to the police officer about what happened. This differs from most other cases where I have a full file of information about the case. As a former prosecutor, I had a burden to prove my case if the case proceeded to trial. The burden of proof is the following beyond a reasonable doubt:

"Willful or wanton disregard" means more than simple carelessness but does not require proof of an intent to cause harm. It means knowingly disregarding the possible risks to the safety of people or property.

Careless Driving on the other hand requires the prosecution to prove you drove in a careless, imprudent or negligent manner. Reckless requires you intentionally drove in a certain manner, whereas Careless doesn't look to your willful disregard but rather the results of your driving.

As a former prosecutor, after speaking to the officer, I needed to decide the strength of my case. I would also look at the driving record of the charged person. Depending on the facts of the case, and the master driving record, I would be open to potentially working out a deal with the defense lawyer. Unfortunately it was rare that a criminal defense lawyer properly laid out the right justification to get the deal done.

Having learned from the mistakes of others, I approach these type of cases in a very different manner. I start with that same ticket issued to my client, but then speak to the client about their version of the case. I understand that my client's version is likely skewed a bit toward a favorable version, and there is a middle ground to what actually happened, because the same applies to the cop; tickets are issued to prosecute.

As a criminal defense lawyer I have to weigh the "asshole factor" of the case. Most cops will cut the driver a break and not issue a Reckless Driving ticket unless something was going on above and beyond the typical case. Was my client actually doing something a lot worse on the road, or did the cop just think my client was an asshole?

We all drive on the same roads and we judge what people do

around us. I've watched people do some crazy things on the road, and think "wow that person is an asshole". It's a quick judgment, but I don't have the full story; I don't know why that person is actually driving that way or where they are going. Same is true for the police officer. They may see my client driving for a 5-10 second clip and hit them with this serious offense.

Cases can also be overcharged out on the road if the cop doesn't like my client for whatever reason. Issuing an overcharged ticket is more common in my experience than submitting a formal charge request to a prosecutor; less checks and balances involved.

My client may have actually fit the parameters of one of these offenses at that moment, but should they suffer the long-term consequences because of that moment in time? I believe it's important to view the case outside the four corners of the ticket; the observation of that police officer is only a very small sample of who my client is within their community, family and in their career. It may also be cop vs client versions with no independent information offered to the defense and prosecution to weigh.

I work with people who need to drive to survive, keep jobs, travel; I even work with many clients in the auto industry who test drive cars for a living!

So what we do is better understand what was actually going on from my client's point of view then we work to take the "asshole factor" off the case. We also acknowledge the perception of our audience and put proactive steps in place to show that this case is a learning opportunity for the client, and a chance to be a better and safer driving going forward. This could mean a driver improvement class, safe driving course, community service, counseling etc. There is no limit to what we can put in place to change the perception of the client's case.

If the cop thinks you're an asshole then he/she is going to relay those thoughts to the prosecutor who will not budge off the charge and invite a trial with a motivated cop on the stand to nail you on the charge. There is a path to keeping your sword away and building consensus in Reckless and Careless Driving cases in Michigan.

If a case comes down to cop vs client, the client is going to struggle to win that trial with the trier of fact. The main goal is to avoid that confrontation and get the police officer to agree with our plan and get the prosecutor to agree. All cases are different, which provide unique challenges, but everyone involved has a degree of common sense, and reaching a consensus which matches your goals is the ultimate outcome for a client going to court on a serious charge.

LEAVING THE SCENE OF AN ACCIDENT

As a former prosecutor, I worked on a lot of Leaving the Scene of an Accident type cases. These charges varied depending upon the facts of the case. The most common was Leaving the Scene of an Accident Causing Property Damage, which simply means the defendant was involved in an accident and drove away. This particular charge carries 6 points on your driving record and is a criminal misdemeanor.

As a former prosecutor, I would talk to the police officer and any witnesses involved to gain a better understanding of the circumstances of this charge. Common inquires for me were the following:

- what time of day did this happen?
- what type of road/area did this occur?
- driving record of the person charged
- if the defendant has a version to share/story to offer up
- how bad was the property damage, nature of the damage
- any efforts by the defendant to stick around/report

It made a big difference if someone with a clean record got into a minor fender bender, stopped, talked to the other driver, and after waiting for the police to arrive, decided they needed to get to work, and they drive off vs someone who destroys ten mailboxes in a neighborhood, smashes into cars and ends up flipped over in someone's yard at 2 am. Sure, both are against the law, but I applied common sense as a prosecutor.

Most defendants in this situation are trying to avoid the points abstracting on their license and avoiding a criminal misdemeanor. There is a 0 point offense called failure to report an accident, which could be the end result in a negotiation; this is still a misdemeanor, but it was a start in resolving a case.

As a prosecutor you have limited resources and time; you must use that time as wisely as possible and pick and choose your hearing and trials. Is the best course of action to take this type of case to trial, or should you focus on making sure all involved are OK, restitution is paid, and assurances (tangible action) the defendant will avoid future issues going forward. Most defense lawyers did not provide the last part when I prosecuted these cases.

While property damage was most common, there is a separate offense for Leaving the Scene of an Accident Causing Personal Injury. This type of case might have similar facts, but another person was injured as part of the case; if the person suffered serious impairment or worse a death, the charges get more serious into the felony level with action on your driver's license.

The misdemeanor "ordinary" injury charge carries 6 points and a 90-day driver's license suspension. Defendant's surely wanted to avoid these sanctions, but when someone was hurt, a lot of that decision depended on input from the injured party.

Having spent time prosecuting these cases, I am well aware of the ins and outs and the options for resolution. If a case is strong, with statements, maybe video, admissions by the defendant if they were located, it's going to be time to try to resolve the case rather than climbing up a steep hill against the evidence. The door is usually open for compromise for these cases.

As stated above, common goals for resolving these cases are to avoid a criminal misdemeanor, points on license and suspension of license. That path varies depending upon the facts of the case. There could be restitution involved for damage to property or injury to a person. Restitution can be challenged with a hearing, but sometimes you can use the agreement not to challenge the restitution to get what you want on the back-end of the deal for your license and record.

While nobody should be leaving the scene of an accident, there is always another side of the story, and if my client has a reason (there is no excuse), we're going to share that story in the best light possible. I may have my client do a driver improvement course, safe driving, community service work etc.

If my client is having mental or emotional issues, and somehow that was a factor in my client leaving the scene, we're going to get into counseling and get a professional involved to show things can be worked on, and my client was not in the best place when this happened.

Anything to provide context and a sign of positive direction for my client. Rather turn the incident into a learning experience than a long-term impact on my client's life.

MALICIOUS DESTRUCTION OF PROPERTY

As a former Michigan prosecutor, I worked on a lot of Malicious Destruction of Property cases, which are usually referred to as MDOP cases. These type of cases can either be a misdemeanor or a felony, which is determined by the amount of damage to the property in question.

If the value is below $200, it is a 93 day misdemeanor

If the value is between $200 and $999 it is a one year misdemeanor

If the value is over $1000, it is a felony offense

As a former prosecutor, I would look for a couple things when evaluating the case.

I would look at the relationship between the two parties; do they know each other?

Is there a possibility that the property could be owned by both parties if they reside together?

Does the accused defendant have a criminal record? How old is this person?

When and where did this happen, and were both parties present?

I saw MDOP cases that ranged from jealous spouses or girlfriends and boyfriends slashing tires or breaking out car windows when the other party was not present, to someone smashing a television or computer in front of the other party, but both parties claim they owned the television or computer.

Many MDOP cases come with additional charges. It was not uncommon to see domestic violence or assault charges along with these MDOP charges. I would always look at the most serious crime, which as a prosecutor would likely be the charge where someone was assaulted rather than property being damaged. Let's assume we're only dealing with the Malicious Destruction of Property charge.

If the defendant was under 24 years old, they might qualify for HYTA, but as the prosecutor, I would need to approve this if the party was 21, 22 or 23 years old. Each prosecutor is different on this policy. If the person was under 21 or under 24, the judge still needs to agree with this outcome.

If the person did not qualify for this program, I might consider a reduction in charges if the victim is made whole and the property is paid for via restitution. This might be a felony MDOP reduced down to a misdemeanor if payment is made as part of the deal. Occasionally, I might even consider a disorderly conduct charge, but I was a very open-minded prosecutor, most prosecutors are not as easy to work with as myself.

As a defense lawyer, I take that experience as a prosecutor and put my client in the best position to show the other side of who they are. To be judged based on a single a police report and incident is the lazy approach to handling a case like this; a poor choice brought on by anger or jealousy is not an excuse, but it is surely the reason. I like to get to the bottom of why my client found themselves in this type of situation. I like to educate the prosecutor on who my client actually is; what they do for a living, their family, their goals and dreams. My clients are human, some get themselves into worse situations than most, but there is always a path to expand the information being considered by the judge and prosecutor.

I've had clients caught red handed destroying property of another, and I have had clients that had no intent or what they did, did not actually create any actual damage, but the other party calls the police and a charge is issued on limited information. I have dealt with broken car windows, smashed laptops, but also cases where my client's sprinkler sprays on a neighbor's yard and they claim some sort of damage was done.

As a defense lawyer, I take the facts in the case and try to position my client in a way where we are already learning and growing from the incident. If my client was in a bad place mentally or emotionally at the time, we're probably in counseling already, if alcohol is involved, we are focusing on insight and awareness and testing for alcohol to show we are sober and have a clear mind going forward. There is always something to do to improve your position when you walk into the courthouse.

If the claim is bogus by the "victim" then we're doing what we can to present the truth in the case. A prosecutor only knows what the police reported in their police reports and what the "victim" claims. It's rare my client had a chance to make a statement, and if they did, the report is tilted in favor of the prosecution, not to my client or they would not be charged to begin with.

We use time to improve a Michigan MDOP case; if we just

relied upon what happened in the heat of the moment then my client is setup to have a criminal record and potentially go to jail. But if we step back, regroup and improve our position, we can go into court and resolve the case while achieving the client's goals.

EXPUNGEMENT

As a former county prosecutor in Michigan, I would typically adopt the position of the Michigan Attorney General who reviews the expungement application and either takes no position or opposes the expungement. For most misdemeanors, it was quite rare that the Attorney General would oppose the motion for expungement, but it did happen on some occasions. If someone is eligible and has not re-offended, the State is pretty good about being on board with a fresh start, but it's by no means a lock.

If a victim was involved it wasn't as clear cut, especially if that victim is still motivated to punish the person with the conviction. If the application for expungement was for a felony, it was a closer call, but if the person successfully completed probation, has not re-offended since the offense, the Michigan Attorney General would usually leave it up to the judge to decide. Most judges as long as nobody is opposing it will typically grant the expungement, but it must be done right from step one. That means preparing for everything.

In the expungement process, the Michigan State Police will produce a review of the applicant's record for eligibility; the Michigan Attorney General receives this information and decides their position then the county/city/township prosecutor will review the Attorney General's position.

Based on my experience as a prosecutor, I have adopted a different, more advanced approach for clients who want to apply for expungement. We follow the same necessary procedure, but we go above and beyond what is necessary; we do more than what was is expected, because we understand that a judge granting expungement is a privilege rather than a right. The judge must decide "is this expungement in the best interest of the community?"

Other than showing the client has not re-offended, I may have my client get re-evaluated by a counselor to provide a real-time update for the prosecutor and judge. I may have the client jump into some additional community service as we highlight all the positive strides the client has made since the incident. I want records of achievements in school, work and life; if the client has been married or had children since the incident, these are key points to bring to the court's attention.

It's my goal to show how the client has grown, learned and improved themselves since the incident; we need to do more than just show they are eligible and haven't been in trouble since the incident. This is your shot at a clean slate and to forego living life as a criminal. I make it clear upfront to a potential client that I am going to make them hustle and work harder than other attorneys.

Some potential clients don't like this process, because they believe the passing of time is enough to justify the result. I know as a prosecutor that it's not as straight forward as some clients believe, and we work to earn the result, and don't assume a single thing. I will only take on a new expungement case if the client understands we will be doing extra work, which is not required, but it is required with me.

RESISTING ARREST

As a former prosecutor, I worked on many resisting arrest cases in both New York City and here in Michigan. The biggest misconception that I had to overcome was the scope of a resisting arrest charge. Most people, even some lawyers viewed resisting arrest as running from the cops, pushing, shoving and not allowing the cops to make an arrest.; straight from the show COPS.

So when I had a case where the facts didn't live up to those images, I received a lot of shoulder shrugs and confusion why such a serious charge. And it is a serious charge; in Michigan resisting arrest is a felony offense, which carries potential prison time. A lot of local townships, cities, villages and other non-county prosecutors charge it as a local ordinance, which is a misdemeanor offense. If the county charges this offense, they have the option of charging it as an attempted resisting arrest, which is a misdemeanor.

In my opinion, one of the worse charges to pop-up on a background check for someone. Not only were you violent, "didn't listen" but you did it with a police officer? Images of punching the cop are front and center for the person seeing this conviction even if those were not the facts.

As a prosecutor, my main concern was my police officer. I was in a position in Oakland County in the Warrants Division and in New York City with the Early Case Assessment Bureau to decide on the particular charge, and depending on the facts, we may go with the felony or the misdemeanor. I had cases where the defendant talked back to the cop, didn't listen and tried to avoid the arrest; this could have been a felony, but many times we went with the attempted resisting and kept the case a misdemeanor.

This was done for many reasons, but one was a sense of fairness/common sense with an eye on felony case management. If the charge had a likelihood of being reduced via plea bargain, we might just start it as a misdemeanor. Why clog up felony prosecutors and the circuit court with borderline felony cases. If the case involved an officer who is injured or attacked beyond some incidental contact, we would most likely go with the felony offense with an eye on potential reduction later on in the case, but that would be up to the police officer.

Resisting arrest cases were usually multi-charge cases meaning the officer(s) were involved for something else then the case also became a resisting arrest incident. DUI, drug possession, domestic violence, disorderly conduct and other offenses were common accompanying charges.

Being on the prosecutor side of the table, I was not impressed with the approach of most of the defense lawyers on these cases. They would come up to me and just ask for a deal on the case; they failed to acknowledge my point of view of the case or how the officer felt about the case.

If the client had no record, they would push this narrative over and over again, and while it is a positive thing the client has no record, they still made some poor choices, and not respecting the police department that my office works with on a daily basis. It's also a pretty strong case when my star witness is a police officer who can offer direct testimony about the incident; I am not relying on a test, science or civilian witnesses. It's a quick and easy trial if I want to go that route.

Based on my experience as a prosecutor, I approach these cases in a very different manner for my clients. I want to avoid a felony, jail time, and potentially keep a conviction off of my client's record. It depends if we're starting with a felony or a misdemeanor and my client's record. We have to acknowledge the perception of our audience (prosecutor and judge). Like a prosecutor, the judge is more familiar and trusting of the local police officer than my client, and I don't ignore that important fact. The general public may also view a police officer as more reliable and trustworthy if they take the stand against my client who may or may not testify at the trial.

It's my goal to present my client in the best light possible for plea negotiations, but not in a bullshit dress them up fashion. If my client has flaws, issues, problems, we put them all on the table. You get no where telling a prosecutor "my client has no record, a family, job and he's a great guy"; it's in one ear and out the other. That is not what a prosecutor is looking for to strike a great deal for the client.

If my client was drunk or high when he allegedly resisted arrest, we're going to focus on substance abuse with proper assessment and evaluation and put a plan into place. We might begin voluntarily daily alcohol testing, jump into alcohol education and/or counseling. If my client was sober, but dealing with emotional or mental health issues, we're going to jump into evaluation on that front and work to address it with properly trained third party professionals. We need to get to the heart of the issue.

The possibilities are endless. Unless my client is just an evil spirit who likes to push around cops and mistreat them, it's likely we're going to be able to figure out why they found themselves on the wrong side of the law. I carefully select my clients on every case, and seek out people with good hearts, who respect their community, but end up on the wrong side of the law due to something going on in their life. I have never worked with someone who I just thought was a bad person looking to hurt people.

The problem is the prosecutor and judge don't know that my client is a good person who is typically a positive person in the community, and makes the right choice 99.9 percent of the time, and can use this as a learning experience vs NEEDING punishment to understand right from wrong.

It's my job to educate and advocate for my client, and again not in a bullshit way. It's ok to be flawed or have a mental, emotional or physical issue that has brought us all together. It actually helps your case if we can point to an issue then work toward resolving or improving that issue.

I get my best results for a client when I fully understand how we ended up working together. A case with some bad facts can quickly turnaround when we identify the variable that caused this case to happen, and we can proactively address for the prosecutor and judge.

I like to approach the case in a way where we are in charge from day one, and actively work on improving the perception and eventually the reality for the prosecutor and judge. These key players have limited time and attention spans to focus on each case; without a comprehensive approach that makes sense, the client will remain a name and a charge. That is how most client's end up with the "default result".

URINATING IN PUBLIC

In Michigan there are a few charges that can be associated with urinating or defecating in public. The more serious route is the State of Michigan offense of Indecent Exposure. In Michigan there is a simple and aggravated indecent exposure when they knowingly make any open or indecent exposure of his or her person to another person.

It becomes the more serious aggravated when the indecent exposure involves fondling yourself or engaging in any sexual acts. Aggravated indecent exposure is essentially masturbating in public, which is a felony offense that carrying a maximum penalty of up to two years in the state prison as well as a fine of up to $2000. Simple indecent exposure is a misdemeanor offense.

Urinating in public could be charged as indecent exposure or it can be charged as a local ordinance as public urinating, which is still a 90-day criminal misdemeanor. The City of Ann Arbor along with other cities, townships and villages have this unique offense on the books.

As a former prosecutor, I would look at the facts of the case before deciding on how to approach and charge the case; I could always amend to a more serious offense or reduce to a less serious offense. Things to consider:

Was the person urinating/exposing themselves in the middle of the day with the intention of people seeing the act, or was it 3 am in a dark alley, but the police catch them?

There's cases of people sitting in the car or in the movie theater exposing themselves; those cases are the indecent exposure cases; peeing in the dark alley or behind the bush after 3 am are the public urination cases in my opinion.

The problem for someone charged, even with the "less serious" version is the perception of that charge on your record; it would be both embarrassing and devastating for your future. Imagine applying for a job or to a graduate school with that offense on your record, how confident do you feel in getting the benefit of the doubt?

I don't ever want a client to leave a case with this offense on their record. Even if we're only charged with the urinating in public and not indecent exposure, we need to be aware that the more serious charge could still be a possibility if a prosecutor amends the charge, because the police officer only issues a ticket, the prosecutor can always add or amend charges.

I would say 99.9 percent of my clients that are charged with urinating in public have been drinking prior to being caught by the police. The clearest way to think about the offense is "would you have done this at 1 pm during your lunch break on a Tuesday?" - if the answer is no (and it typically is), then the alcohol is why this happened. I've never had a client who urinates in public because they think its acceptable and a good way to approach life; they drink a bit too much and they simply don't properly weigh the consequences of their actions.

They assume (and they would normally be right) that they will get away with it, they really HAVE TO GO and it's worth the risk. Reflecting back, they of course admit it was not a wise choice, and they wish they HELD IT or found another means to go to the bathroom.

In reality there are worse things to do when you've had too much to drink. Peeing in public is unacceptable and against the law, but there are means to resolve this type of case without this charge branding you forever. Assuming my client drank too much, there may be other charges associated with urinating, such as an MIP, fake ID, disorderly conduct etc. Let's simplify it and assume we are only charged with the UIP.

The best way in my opinion to get at the heart of the issue is to address the alcohol consumption. If my client made this choice due in part to the alcohol consumption, well they probably drank too much and it impacted the way they would normally behave (back to that lunch time example).

I may have a client attend an AA meeting or two, write a reflection piece to gain some additional insight into how alcohol can lead to bad choices that then lead to criminal charges. We might take an alcohol insight and awareness course, see a counselor for a session, and may even jump into a day or two of volunteer work. We need to take the STINK off the case and show who the client actually is; someone who can reflect upon a poor choice in life, grow and learn from it, and go forward and make better choices.

When a client goes to court, the only thing the prosecutor and judge knows about the client is their name, age, and what they are charged with; not a favorable pool of information to get the best result; this is the first impression. I try to create a TRUE impression for my client's - highlight who my client is outside of this incident, and show that additional reflection back on the incident, steps they have taken to address the issue and where they are going in the future with a better mindset.

MINOR IN POSSESSION

In 2018, a Minor in Possession charge is now a civil infraction. Prior to this year, this offense was a criminal misdemeanor. That seems like good news for my clients, and it sounded great to the lawmakers who created the law, but things are NOT playing out in a favorable way for people in Michigan. Yes, it is a win for someone not to have a criminal record for underage drinking, but there are a ton of collateral consequences, many of these issues, which I am fixing for people who screwed up their own case or received poor advice from other lawyers.

Prior to 2018, if you were charged with an MIP, you would likely plead guilty under a first offender program, do some probation, pay a fine, and your record is clear with no paper trail of the offense. Your case was non-public and you did not have to report it as a criminal conviction. Now, people are going into court, pleading responsible to the civil infraction of Minor in Possession, but this is a public record. Very public, just like a traffic ticket.

Sure it's not a criminal case, but it comes up and the facts/evidence are not any different. It's also a crime in most states, and I have had a client plead responsible to the civil infraction in Michigan, but his home state still suspended his license for 12 months, because that state still considered it a criminal offense. I've had clients get fired from a job because their employer had this on their record, and the employer didn't care if it was a crime or not, it just meant the same to them - breaking the law with alcohol.

This same logic would certainly apply to a grad school, employer, a scholarship committee etc. Let's evaluate someone who received an MIP in 2017 vs 2018.

In 2017, in a reasonable worse case scenario, the person would go on probation on the first offender program, excel, have the case dismissed, and the arrest/charge and plea would all be non-public. On applications there would be no need to put the offense, and there would be no record of it at the courthouse or on a public database. This person is safe from their past impacting their future plans.

In 2018, a Minor in Possession pops up in that same search, and most applications ask for any civil infractions in your past; that means you would need to list it and explain what happened. Now the person who sees that might say - "isn't an MIP a crime?" Or, it says civil infraction, but do I really want to hire or admit someone who "breaks the law?" - even one incident of underage drinking could send the wrong perception to the person reviewing the record.

They can easy then FOIA the police report connected to the MIP case, and there could be some embarrassing facts in there as a college kid charged with underage drinking. There could even be some facts about other crimes that are under first offender programs, or crimes not charged, but the facts could support them. Common other crimes that go with an MIP might be possessing a fake ID, urinating in public, disorderly conduct, disturbing the peace, public intoxication, open container etc.

As a former prosecutor, I understand the typical prosecutor mindset of "well he/she already caught a break" or "it's not even a crime". This can be frustrating to hear, and it's so shortsighted.

Most prosecutors DO NOT think outside the box and they don't understand or consider collateral consequences. That's like me saying well there's a gas leak at my house, and they say, well the house isn't on fire, what's the big deal? Sure, in the moment it's a civil infraction, but once that record becomes public it sets off fireworks in all directions for the client., and you can run from it, because it's not eligible for expungement This is why I have not allowed any of my clients charged with an MIP to walk into the courthouse and plead responsible.

I approach these cases as if the offense is still a serious criminal offense, and value the fact that my client should not be underage drinking, and we can learn from this. We over prepare and outwork the others charged wit hthe same offense.

To simply ignore what happened will only lead to the client piling up MIP's and getting into more trouble with alcohol in the immediate future, and down the road as they get older. It's my goal to workout an alternative outcome with the prosecutor that is NOT an MIP.

This could be accomplished in many ways; we can turn the MIP into a different civil infraction, which won't pop up as an alcohol offense; this would be the optimal result, but not always offered by a prosecutor. That is why my client's go above and beyond with a proactive approach to push the limits on negotiations, and give me the currency I need to make things happen.

FAKE ID

As a former prosecutor in both New York City and Michigan, I worked on many fraudulent identification cases. I use that term rather than FAKE ID, because it's a more serious crime than many people want to believe. Most people think of this offense as trying to enter a bar or buy some beer at the corner store, and the bouncer or store owner takes the ID and tells you to get lost. If it were that simple, there would be no criminal charges.

Although 99.9 percent of the FAKE ID cases I handle do involve an underage person "just getting caught", the charge itself does not read the same way on paper. I say this because the perception of the case far outweighs the reality of the situation. Prosecutors are pretty reasonable on FAKE ID cases in Michigan if approached in the correct manner, but they also don't understand how the case looks from an outsider.

If you're charged with this offense, here is what the offense actually says under MCL 28.295 It states, in part, "that no one shall intentionally reproduce, alter, counterfeit, forge, or duplicate an official state identification card or use an official state identification card that has been reproduced, altered, counterfeited, forged or duplicated."

You do not want a potential employer, grad school or anyone else seeing this on your record. Forging? Counterfeit? Altering government documents? No no no. Going to medical school, law school, want to be a CPA, a teacher, a nurse? Would you hire or admit someone into those fields who alters government documents?

If the crime read "possessed an identification card to enter a bar or buy alcohol, because the defendant is a good student in college, but still can't legally buy it" then OK - taking some liberties there, but the charge doesn't say anything like that, because the FAKE ID for alcohol is only a small portion of this criminal offense. I don't allow my clients or sometimes their parents to ignore the serious consequences of this charge; it is a lot more than having a "FAKE ID" at the bar.

As a criminal defense lawyer I take an aggressive and immediate approach to this charge. This does not mean we aggressively "fight the case", because if you were caught with the ID trying to get the bar then you were caught with it - what's your defense? There's a misconception when charged with a crime that you should get out your sword and do battle; what if you're really guilty, why would you pull out your sword to be slaughtered? Many lawyers try to sell this approach to clients, but it's foolish, and puts the client in a terrible position with the prosecutor, and potentially the charge.

There's many paths to take for a case like this, and I have found the path of building consensus and peacemaking to the best approach, especially on a charge where the prosecutor is going to be open to resolution. If you storm the prosecutor's castle on day one with your sword, those options aren't going to be there.

The first thing we do is acknowledge the perception of our audience. If charged with a FAKE ID type case, well you're also going to be "charged" in the prosecutor's mind with underage drinking - officially or unofficially - why else would you have the ID on your person?

We treat the case in two parts. We address the alcohol issue, and put items into place to gain further insight and awareness about choices with alcohol. No, it is not a crime anymore in Michigan to underage drink, but that does not matter to a prosecutor, we need to show we're willing to learn from the incident. We also need to work on practicing heightened awareness and properly weighing the consequences of our actions, especially when it's so easy to try to get away with something. Take a step back, reflect and acknowledge the poor choice.

We may do things like alcohol classes, attend an AA meeting with reflection essay, and a day or two of community service. Better to put the case on a pedestal and treat it like a serious matter that we need to address rather than blowing it of as if it's not a big deal. I put my clients through the paces to provide enough currency to resolve these cases with the prosecutor.

If the client shows "they give a crap" and respect the charge and the incident then a prosecutor and judge will be more open to keeping this serious charge off of their record. This means more than saying "I'm sorry" or "I will never do this again" - that's a ton of hot and useless air being wasted in court. Real actions and credibility are all that matters to a prosecutor.

Take it lightly, and show you haven't learned a single thing then maybe you should be stuck with this on you record; I strongly believe in the opposite - take it serious and learn from it even if it takes more work.

TRAVEL REQUESTS

In Michigan, a defendant needs permission of the court and/or probation to travel outside of the State of Michigan or to leave the country during probation and during bond.

As a former New York City and Michigan prosecutor, I was on the other side of many travel requests from defendants. While I generally left the decision up to the judge, I was often asked by the judge what my position on the matter was - this puts a young prosecutor in a tough position, because a prosecutor brings the charge against the defendant, but isn't necessarily in a good position to determine if someone should be able to travel during a criminal case.

The problem is most young prosecutors are blinded by their role and believe they must argue against whatever the other attorney is requesting. This is a very silly and unnecessary thing to do, but most prosecutors don't have a ton of common sense. As a former prosecutor I would generally tell the judge "we leave that to the discretion of the court" rather than agreeing or disagreeing. If the prosecutor responses with a "NO, they shouldn't travel" then the judge is in a spot where he needs to decide for one side, rather than agreeing to something both parties are in agreement. Some prosecutors just don't know how to agree to something even if its the reasonable thing to do.

As someone who works with clients now, I take this experience and make sure that I speak to the prosecutor before making my request to the judge. I anticipate the judge probing the prosecutor for a response, and instead of relying on that prosecutor reacting in a reasonable way when surprised on the spot, I give them a heads up and run it by them. As long as my client is not currently in violation of bond conditions or giving a reason to be concerned, the prosecutor will usually agree "sure, that's fine with me, I don't oppose". That way if the judge does ask, the prosecutor is already thinking about it, and doesn't need to respond with a rash and quick answer that might jam my client up.

Based on my experience as a prosecutor, I have also developed a proactive approach to all cases, which I discuss in great detail in other writings, books and articles. This approach is essential in assisting my clients gain permission to travel out of the state or country during a pending criminal case. If my client is charged with a drug or alcohol offense, we have already been testing more than most are required, and if its alcohol, we are likely on a portable unit, which gives the judge every reason to allow travel. My clients are typically already in counseling, education programs and on the right path during the case; they have earned a bit of the benefit of the doubt and risk losing that benefit if they run into issue while traveling.

Lesson is don't assume a judge and prosecutor will apply common sense or give you the benefit of the doubt. Even if the travel is for work, a family wedding, something "required", that doesn't mean you will be allowed to go.

Plan in advance, talk about it with your lawyer and make sure you're doing something than just asking in order to get permission. Show the judge and prosecutor you deserve that permission, don't assume you'll receive it.

DISORDERLY CONDUCT

As a former Michigan and New York City prosecutor, I worked on hundreds of disorderly conduct cases. In the grand scheme of things this type of charge was on the very bottom of criminal charges, but it is still a crime, and should be taken very seriously. When the question of "do you have a criminal record" is asked, the answer is YES just like it would be for more serious offenses.

Disorderly conduct was a bit of a catch-all charge for criminal activity that did not fit into another category. It was also a type of charge that might be offered as a plea reduction down from a more serious charge. One common reduction would be a retail fraud charge, which is then converted into the amended charge of disorderly conduct - this would avoid the "crime of theft, fraud and dishonesty"

In Michigan the term "disorderly person" covers a broad range of undesirable behavior, including:

- being able-bodied but failing to support your family
- being a prostitute or "loitering" (hanging out) in places of prostitution
- being a "Peeping Tom"
- engaging in an illegal business or profession (such as illegal gambling)
- loitering in places where illegal business is transacted
- being intoxicated in public and disturbing others or endangering people or property
- engaging in indecent or obscene conduct in public (such as nudity or sexual acts)
- being a vagrant

- loitering at police stations, jails, hospitals, or courthouses, soliciting work as an attorney or bail bond, and
- unnecessarily jostling or crowding others in public places.

I would say 95 percent of the disorderly conduct charges that a prosecutor works with is the final charge - the jostling or crowding others in a public place, because this is a common reduction charge - you would not reduce retail fraud to a "peeing tom" disorderly conduct.

Being a disorderly person is punishable by up to 90 days in jail, a fine of up to $500, or both. Funeral picketing is a felony, punishable by up to two years in prison, a fine of up to $5,000, or both. Subsequent convictions are punishable by up to four years in prison or a fine of up to $10,000, or both.

As a defense lawyer it's rare to see a lone disorderly orderly conduct charge; it typically comes along with other charges, usually alcohol offenses. The above definition and categories are State of Michigan offenses, but this is a common charge on the city, township, village and municipal level.

Disorderly conduct is a very valuable tool as a criminal lawyer, because it is the best type of reduction for a client from a more serious misdemeanor. And because it is a 90 day misdemeanor vs a one year or 93 day misdemeanor, it avoids many of the issues with the more serious offenses. I have had clients resolve their cases with a 90-day misdemeanor, and it does not show up on a background check. I have had prosecutors tell me the same, because fingerprints are not required for 90 day offenses, which helps prevent tracking/paper trail.

As a criminal defense lawyer, I have petitioned courts to get fingerprints back along with arrest cards if my client was first prosecuted for a more serious offense then it is reduced to disorderly conduct.

It is quite the challenge to convince a prosecutor to take a more serious charge and reduce it down to disorderly conduct because of the "less serious offense" issue - to think it may not come up in a background check discourages many prosecutors from offering. It's a bit of a holy grail outcome for many serious cases.

I have even had DUI offenses in Michigan reduced down to disorderly conduct. It's not a common outcome, but my clients have earned that exceptional outcome by being proactive, and changing the perception of their case. If we can change the hearts and minds of the prosecutor and judge, anything is possible when charged with a crime.

OPEN CONTAINER

As a former prosecutor in both New York City and Michigan, I worked on many open container charges. In Michigan there is a state law for open containers in a vehicle, but not necessarily outside of a vehicle.

In Michigan, a person who is an operator or occupant shall not transport or possess alcoholic liquor in a container that is open or uncapped or upon which the seal is broken within the passenger area of a vehicle upon a highway, or within the passenger area of a moving vehicle in any place open to the general public or generally accessible to motor vehicles, including an area designated for the parking of vehicles, in this state.

A person who violates this section is guilty of a misdemeanor. As part of the sentence, the person may be ordered to perform community service and undergo substance abuse screening and assessment at his or her own expense.

As a former prosecutor, I was not thinking about how this type of offense could impact the person charged, because this type of case can never be expunged because it is under the Michigan Vehicle Code and not the penal code. It cannot be taken under HYTA or 771.1 so a prosecutor isn't doing someone any favors with this charge. It's possible to run into a prosecutor who simply says "no deals" then you're in trouble, because a trial on the issue might not be fruitful if the evidence is clear and strong. So what do you do?

As a criminal defense lawyer, I know that most of my clients are not in a good position when it comes to the evidence against them, so we need to think outside of the box. Pulling out your sword to fight a strong case is only setting my client up for failure - there needs to be another way. I work the proactive and moral approach. What if a prosecutor says no deal?

First you acknowledge the perception of your audience. Having an open container in a vehicle is dangerous and can lead to drunk driving, injury, death etc. As long as the client is not also changed with a DUI, there is some room for turning the facts into a valuable lesson learned situation.

Doubling down on alcohol insight and awareness, jumping into a handful of AA meetings, maybe taking a safe driving course - anything to further ingrain positive life choices, especially when it comes to alcohol and where alcohol is consumed, transported and possessed.

We need to show the prosecutor that we understand what happened is not acceptable, and take control of the situation and take action on our own. We stand a better chance convincing a prosecutor to weigh the pros and cons of a criminal conviction for the rest of my client's life in our favor if we have this currency to play. It's also not bullshit; walking into the prosecutor's office and saying "my client can't have a record" is a load of crap and worthless - it might work with some prosecutors, but not the prosecutor who says NO DEAL.

You need to come to court already two steps ahead of that prosecutor and blow them away. Better to work to change perceptions before going to court than asking a prosecutor to buy into your case the day of court with nothing to back it.

My goal for a client charged with the State of Michigan open container offense is to reduce the case to a civil infraction or the very least a different charge outside of the Michigan Vehicle Code that can be dismissed under a first offender type program.

Along with the State of Michigan open container in a vehicle charge, many cities, villages, townships and municipalities have this type of charge for an open container on a public street. While this does not involve a vehicle, it may be more serious for someone under 21 - even if the client is over 21, this is a criminal charge, which would give my client a criminal record.

It would be our goal to take the same approach as above and put a number of proactive steps into place before going to court to work toward a resolution where the charge does not end up on my client's record.

EMBEZZLEMENT

As a former prosecutor in New York City and Michigan, I worked on many embezzlement cases. In Michigan, embezzlement is defined as someone in control of the money or property of another person or of a business, and are accused of converting the money for your own use or fraudulently disposing of the money.

This is different than larceny, retail fraud, home invasion and other theft crimes because embezzlement means you're legally possessing or controlling the money at the time, but you commit a crime when you convert the money to your own benefit. Retail fraud is shopping at Kohl's and taking a shirt without paying for it; embezzlement is working at Kohl's and creating gift cards for yourself or stealing money from the register.

In Michigan, embezzlement can either me a misdemeanor or a felony - the differing factor is the amount of value converted for your own good. Here are the penalties

Embezzlement of money or property valued at less that $200 (misdemeanor): Jail time of up to 93 days and a fine of either $500 or 3 times the value of the money or property, whichever is greater.

Embezzlement of money or property valued at between $200 and $1,000, or less than $200 with a previous embezzlement conviction, or under $200 embezzled from a nonprofit or charitable organization (misdemeanor): Jail time of up to 1 year and a fine of either $1,000, or 3 times the value of the money or property, whichever is greater.

Embezzlement of money or property valued at between $1,000 and $20,000, or between $200 and $1,000 along with a previous conviction, or between $200 and $1,000 embezzled from a nonprofit or charitable organization (felony): Jail time of up to 5 years and a fine of up to $10,000, or 3 times the value of the money or property, whichever is greater.

Embezzlement of money or property valued at between $20,000 and $50,000, or between $1,000 and $20,000 along with a previous conviction, or between $1,000 and $20,000 embezzled from a nonprofit or charitable organization (felony): Jail time of up to 10 years and a fine of $15,000 or 3 times the value of the money or property, whichever is greater.

Embezzlement of money or property valued at between $50,000 and $100,000 (felony): Jail time of up to 15 years and a fine of $25,000 or 3 times the value of the money or property, whichever is greater.

Embezzlement of money or property valued at more than $100,000 (felony): Jail time of up to 20 years and a fine of up to $50,000 or 3 times the value of the money or property, whichever is greater.

As a prosecutor my number one concern was always my "victim" and making my victim whole again. If the person charge stole $1500 worth of value from the victim, my top goal was to get that victim back the $1500. From there I would focus on the punishment of the defendant, but not without considering my victim first.

If the person charge lacked a criminal record, there may be

room for negotiations in order to recoup the money from the defendant. I was more likely to gain a return of that money if I was willing to deal down from a felony to a misdemeanor or potentially deal to a dismissal altogether. Prosecutors see black and white when it comes to charges - they don't really consider what each type of charge means in the real world. An embezzlement conviction on someone's record is about the worse thing for ever getting a job or passing a background check.

I use my experience as a former prosecutor and get inside the mind of the other side. I realize that the prosecutor is likely most concerned about the financial return to their victim. If after reviewing all of the evidence it appears the prosecutor has a strong case, we may shift positions and focus on a number of goals such as avoiding jail, a felony, and maybe a criminal record altogether.

I don't just rely on my client writing a check to the victim to get the deal done, because this will only get us part of the way toward our goals. We need to acknowledge the perception of our audience and realize that my client was in a position of trust and ripped off someone who trusted them - either an individual person or a company.

Is the prosecutor really going to give them a slap on the wrist and push them out of the courthouse door without any record of this happening for others to be fooled in the future? Probably not.

It's very important to get to the bottom of the issue with the client and try to figure out how they went from being a trusted person to throwing that trust out the window and defrauding someone else. What's going on in my client's mental, emotional and physical state? Is there something new that triggered this poor choice?

It could be family issues, alcohol/drugs, stress, work related, financial; whatever it is, we are going to identify it and put my client in a position to work on the issue and hopefully fix it. We can't ask for the best outcome without solving the problem on our own.

If we can present why this happened, and a solution, a prosecutor and judge don't need to worry about pushing my client out the door as a serious threat to society. There is an opportunity for a true second chance, but it needs to make sense to the prosecutor and judge, and the way to do that is with actions, not mere words.

LARCENY

As a former prosecutor, I worked on many larceny cases; the most confusing part of this charge for many defendants and even defense lawyers is the difference between general larceny and retail fraud.

When an individual takes another person's property, they have committed the crime of larceny.
Michigan's general larceny statute prohibits the stealing of certain types of property including: money, goods, bank notes, deeds, receipts, public records, and scrap metal. The law also criminalizes larceny conducted by entering or breaking into a motor vehicle or trailer and by removing or taking away certain motor vehicle parts. Larceny offenses are categorized as either a misdemeanor or felony depending on the value amount of the stolen property.

These are items that are NOT FOR SALE. If you walk into a retail store and steal a pair of socks that is retail fraud; you steal someone's laptop at Starbucks that's considered to be larceny.

In Michigan, if the stolen property has a value of less than $200, the offense is punishable by imprisonment for not more than 93 days and/or a fine not to exceed $500 or 3x the value of the stolen property, whichever is greater.

If the stolen property is valued at $200 or more, but less than $1,000, the offense is punishable by imprisonment of not more than 1 year and/or a fine of not more than $2,000 or 3x the value of the stolen property, whichever is greater.
If the value of the items is $1000 or more then it is a felony offense.

The above are State of Michigan offenses, which has a separate retail fraud offense; if you are charged by a city, township, village or other municipality, the traditional retail fraud could be listed as larceny - it can be confusing.

When I evaluated larceny cases as a former prosecutor, I would look at the relationship between the parties, the value, the item itself and how it happened. I would be looking for the level of intrusion on the victim; it would make a difference to me if the defendant stole the item in the presence of the victim vs the defendant taking some scrap metal from the property of the victim.

I might give someone the benefit of the doubt if they "stole something" that could have been interpreted as abandoned vs an obvious "hey you're stealing directly from someone"

I would look at the defendant's record and I would hope that the defense lawyer had some backstory of further information for me to evaluate. If all they have for me is "my client is a great person, he has a job, family" then they aren't going to do any better than the default outcome that everyone else receives.

As a defense lawyer, I take my experience as a prosecutor and always look to better understand how my client found themselves charged with this serious crime. It's my job as a lawyer to work with my client to make sense of why this happened; if the only information available is the police report, well then my client is just a bad person and a crook who steals - it doesn't matter what they do for a living, their family situation or why this happened.

I might have my client work with a counselor to talk about the case, and identify how we got here - we put a plan in place to work on our issues and show a prosecutor and judge that we're not going to walk away from the case as a threat to society without learning anything.

If they believe that then my client is not going to get the outcome we're looking to achieve. Handle your issue proactively, set the stage for how the future looks for your client, and there is room to resolve a case like this with a great result.

The prosecutor and judge think you're a thief who rips people off with no concerns for their happiness or well-being if we don't add something different to the story outside of the police report and the allegations.

DUI FIRST OFFENSE

As a former prosecutor in New York City and Michigan, I had very different experiences in these roles. In New York City, defendants would typically receive quick reductions down to non-misdemeanors, with a very limited if any license suspension and rarely did a first offender receive any probation. In Michigan, drunk driving cases were handled a lot differently.

In Michigan, a drunk driving case can really vary depending upon what police department makes the arrest, because it determines what courthouse the case is heard, an who the prosecutor on the case is going to be. Some prosecutors are quick to reduce Operating While Intoxicated or Super Drunk charges down to Impaired Driving, but rarely anything below this offer. Judges typically put people on at least 12 months of probation, and some courts do send first offenders to jail.

Prosecutors typically view DUI cases as serious charges, and pretty straight forward to prosecute. Prosecutors look for evidence of driving the car then the chemical test result being over the legal limit. If they have evidence of both of those, they are confident in their case, and typically hold firm in standard offers to the defendant.

Some prosecutors have "policies" and will not make offers or will play hard ball day one, inviting a trial if you don't like the offer. The majority of prosecutors don't want to set DUI's for trial and make themselves much busier; they have large caseloads and want to resolve cases.

Most prosecutors will give some benefit of the doubt to someone with no prior DUI convictions, but will look harshly upon accidents, poor driving, an exceptionally high BAC number, and any funny business in terms of acting poorly toward the police officers. If the case is a clean traffic stop, a relatively common BAC number, there's likely to be an opening offer that might be appealing to some defendants.

As a criminal defense attorney I don't want to settle for the default/"what everyone else gets" result. I want to create more options for my client, and we do that by creating leverage both outside and inside the courtroom.

We create leverage outside of the courtroom by being proactive and changing the perception of the case from day one. When the case begins depending on your record, the prosecutor and judge will view you as a dangerous drunk driver who is lucky to not have killed someone.

As a criminal defense lawyer I anticipate the perception of my audience and look to expand the information pool with positive information about my client's past, present and future. When I say information, I don't just mean telling the prosecutor my client has a good job, a family and he's a nice guy. The information comes from real action, which begins with a substance abuse evaluation with a follow-up on recommendations.

The majority of my DUI clients are not frequent drinkers, they typically don't have more than 2-3 drinks, and have no criminal record. They have good jobs, pay their taxes, respect the law, and agree that drunk driving is not a good thing, and there should be punishment for the crime. They find themselves facing a DUI charge unexpectedly due to some variable changing on the day of the offense.

It usually stems from not planning ahead, because my client has no intention of drinking too much. The night begins without plans in place, and the environment, surroundings, people involved are different than expected, and my client drinks more than usual, and they are unfamiliar with this situation, and don't put the breaks on. The drinks keep flowing and those drinks impact positive decisions. The client's decisions are no longer completely their own and they trick themselves into believing "risking it" is a good trade off to leaving a car in a parking lot, missing an early doctors appointment or their kids little league game. They make the decision to drive, because the chances are more likely they get home ok without incident.

They fail to weigh the consequences, even if smaller and less likely - what if I get caught? Worse, what if I kill someone?

If we can make this situation make sense to a prosecutor and judge, we're going to get a lot further along in our case. Essentially we can isolate this poor choice and get away from any perception that this is typical behavior, an addiction, something we can't control. If we can pinpoint how we got there and work on that, a prosecutor and judge will view my client in a different light.

Overcoming the "dangerous drunk driver" perception starts with identifying the true issue, demonstrating that you're taking it seriously, and ready and willing to work on it. With the evaluation comes a recommendation, which is usually counseling, alcohol education, Impact Weekend, AA attendance. We do proactive community service, MADD panels and most importantly daily alcohol testing. Yes, we voluntarily begin alcohol testing, because we need to show that alcohol is not a friend, and it's not something we rely on, we're dependent on, and rather than say "I learned a lot, I don't even a want to drink", we go ahead and show it.

This is how we create leverage outside of the courtroom. I've used this leverage to turn DUI cases into non-DUI cases, probation cases into non-probation cases, and saved people's career, family and possibly their life. Prosecutor's don't like to go outside of the box, but if they do, it will require currency to justify their decision.

Being proactive outside of the courtroom is going to lead to better deals with the prosecutor, and more favorable sentences from probation and the judge, but the best outcomes also have leverage inside of the courtroom, which means we need to find something within the facts of the case to push the buttons of the prosecutor a bit - create some sort of holes or uncertainly in the case.

As a defense lawyer I view DUI cases within three windows:

1. The traffic stop
2. The arrest
3. Chemical tests

Traffic stop requires reasonable suspicion, an arrest require probable cause, and chemical tests must be done correctly to be admissible against my client. A full review of reports, videos, audio, and other evidence will hopefully provide us something to work with in terms of creating leverage. This could mean leverage for pretrial motion or at trial.

Defeating the stop could mean everything after the stop is

inadmissible. Showing the arrest was not based on probable cause could suppress any field sobriety, statements, and chemical tests. Suppressing the blood or breath test could leave a prosecutor quite thin on evidence for trial.

The goal is not necessarily to file the motion or set for trial, because that runs the risk of losing control of the outcome or losing a plea offer, but having the leverage to proceed with either option - something more than a blanket "I'll set for motion or trial" - that's a bluff and prosecutors do not bite on those. You need to show them the leverage in a reasonable way - don't pull out your sword, just talk about the sword a bit.

Win with consensus, work toward a compromise that works for everyone. I've had prosecutors offer disorderly conduct and dismiss drunk driving because it was the right outcome, but I needed both the leverage within the evidence of the case, and my client needed to back it up outside of the courtroom.

DUI SECOND OFFENSE

Here are some unique thoughts on a second offense, and what might be different about the approach below.

With a second offense comes mandatory jail time and potential loss of driver's license for a full year. You certainly don't have the benefit of the doubt with a prior DUI offense on your record. The only benefit of the doubt could be the first DUI is from 20-25 years ago vs someone who has their second DUI in 2-3 years.

A second could bring sobriety court into play, which could allow my client to avoid jail and potentially keep their ability to drive, but not all courts have sobriety courts, and not all clients will qualify.

The proactive program is even more intense for a client with a prior DUI offense. We lose a bit of the approach that we're pinpointing an isolated reason why this happened - we can't sell that because this is the second time it has happened now. You can try to blame the lack of attention to the issue round one, and now "you're finally getting help" now but your audience is less receptive.

I typically lean more toward intensive counseling, getting help, admitting you have a problem - even if it's only been the two times you drank too much, you don't get the benefit of the doubt.

Below you will see my detailed thoughts on drunk driving cases from both the prosecutor viewpoint and the criminal defense side of the case.

As a former prosecutor, I had very little patience for a second offender, and most prosecutors believe the same thing, but leverage still matters. Poke holes in a prosecutor's case and well the prior offense isn't going to make the second case any stronger. If anything a prosecutor may try to come up with a compromise to make sure the defendant is at least on probation and being monitored. Those holes need to be backed up with currency outside of the courtroom so a prosecutor can justify "dismissing a DUI" when the person has a prior - that's a lot to swallow as a prosecutor and risky in the political world.

As a former prosecutor in New York City and Michigan, I had very different experiences in these roles. In New York City, defendants would typically receive quick reductions down to non-misdemeanors, with a very limited if any license suspension and rarely did a first offender receive any probation. In Michigan, drunk driving cases were handled a lot differently.

In Michigan, a drunk driving case can really vary depending upon what police department makes the arrest, because it determines what courthouse the case is heard, an who the prosecutor on the case is going to be. Some prosecutors are quick to reduce Operating While Intoxicated or Super Drunk charges down to Impaired Driving, but rarely anything below this offer. Judges typically put people on at least 12 months of probation, and some courts do send first offenders to jail.

Prosecutors typically view DUI cases as serious charges, and pretty straight forward to prosecute. Prosecutors look for evidence of driving the car then the chemical test result being over the legal limit. If they have evidence of both of those, they are confident in their case, and typically hold firm in standard offers to the defendant.

Some prosecutors have "policies" and will not make offers or will play hard ball day one, inviting a trial if you don't like the offer. The majority of prosecutors don't want to set DUI's for trial and make themselves much busier; they have large caseloads and want to resolve cases.

Most prosecutors will give some benefit of the doubt to someone with no prior DUI convictions, but will look harshly upon accidents, poor driving, an exceptionally high BAC number, and any funny business in terms of acting poorly toward the police officers. If the case is a clean traffic stop, a relatively common BAC number, there's likely to be an opening offer that might be appealing to some defendants.

As a criminal defense attorney I don't want to settle for the default/"what everyone else gets" result. I want to create more options for my client, and we do that by creating leverage both outside and inside the courtroom.

We create leverage outside of the courtroom by being proactive and changing the perception of the case from day one. When the case begins depending on your record, the prosecutor and judge will view you as a dangerous drunk driver who is lucky to not have killed someone.

As a criminal defense lawyer I anticipate the perception of my audience and look to expand the information pool with positive information about my client's past, present and future. When I say information, I don't just mean telling the prosecutor my client has a good job, a family and he's a nice guy. The information comes from real action, which begins with a substance abuse evaluation with a follow-up on recommendations.

The majority of my DUI clients are not frequent drinkers, they typically don't have more than 2-3 drinks, and have no criminal record. They have good jobs, pay their taxes, respect the law, and agree that drunk driving is not a good thing, and there should be punishment for the crime. They find themselves facing a DUI charge unexpectedly due to some variable changing on the day of the offense.

It usually stems from not planning ahead, because my client has no intention of drinking too much. The night begins without plans in place, and the environment, surroundings, people involved are different than expected, and my client drinks more than usual, and they are unfamiliar with this situation, and don't put the breaks on. The drinks keep flowing and those drinks impact positive decisions. The client's decisions are no longer completely their own and they trick themselves into believing "risking it" is a good trade off to leaving a car in a parking lot, missing an early doctors appointment or their kids little league game. They make the decision to drive, because the chances are more likely they get home ok without incident.

They fail to weigh the consequences, even if smaller and less likely - what if I get caught? Worse, what if I kill someone?

If we can make this situation make sense to a prosecutor and judge, we're going to get a lot further along in our case. Essentially we can isolate this poor choice and get away from any perception that this is typical behavior, an addiction, something we can't control. If we can pinpoint how we got there and work on that, a prosecutor and judge will view my client in a different light.

Overcoming the "dangerous drunk driver" perception starts with identifying the true issue, demonstrating that you're taking it seriously, and ready and willing to work on it. With the evaluation comes a recommendation, which is usually counseling, alcohol education, Impact Weekend, AA attendance. We do proactive community service, MADD panels and most importantly daily alcohol testing. Yes, we voluntarily begin alcohol testing, because we need to show that alcohol is not a friend, and it's not something we rely on, we're dependent on, and rather than say "I learned a lot, I don't even a want to drink", we go ahead and show it.

This is how we create leverage outside of the courtroom. I've used this leverage to turn DUI cases into non-DUI cases, probation cases into non-probation cases, and saved people's career, family and possibly their life. Prosecutor's don't like to go outside of the box, but if they do, it will require currency to justify their decision.

Being proactive outside of the courtroom is going to lead to better deals with the prosecutor, and more favorable sentences from probation and the judge, but the best outcomes also have leverage inside of the courtroom, which means we need to find something within the facts of the case to push the buttons of the prosecutor a bit - create some sort of holes or uncertainly in the case. As a defense lawyer I view DUI cases within three windows:

1. The traffic stop
2. The arrest

3. Chemical tests

Traffic stop requires reasonable suspicion, an arrest require probable cause, and chemical tests must be done correctly to be admissible against my client. A full review of reports, videos, audio, and other evidence will hopefully provide us something to work with in terms of creating leverage. This could mean leverage for pretrial motion or at trial.

Defeating the stop could mean everything after the stop is inadmissible. Showing the arrest was not based on probable cause could suppress any field sobriety, statements, and chemical tests. Suppressing the blood or breath test could leave a prosecutor quite thin on evidence for trial.

The goal is not necessarily to file the motion or set for trial, because that runs the risk of losing control of the outcome or losing a plea offer, but having the leverage to proceed with either option - something more than a blanket "I'll set for motion or trial" - that's a bluff and prosecutors do not bite on those. You need to show them the leverage in a reasonable way - don't pull out your sword, just talk about the sword a bit.

Win with consensus, work toward a compromise that works for everyone. I've had prosecutors offer disorderly conduct and dismiss drunk driving because it was the right outcome, but I needed both the leverage within the evidence of the case, and my client needed to back it up outside of the courtroom.

DUI THIRD OFFENSE

Here are some unique thoughts on a third offense, and what might be different about the approach below.

In Michigan, a third offense is a felony, and there is no timeline to get outside of this window. A DUI conviction at 18, 38 and 68 is still a felony. The Secretary of State still uses the 3 in 10 rule, so under this scenario, your driver's license would be impacted as a first offender, and not a third offender.

A third offense DUI in Michigan comes with a mandatory 30 jail sentence with a maximum of 5 years in prison. Most DUI third offenses will carry a jail term of 30 days to 6 months depending on the judge.

As a former prosecutor who worked on felony DUI cases there is very little room for sympathy for the defendant. Most prosecutors will not deal and will just say "set it for trial", but there are some counties in Michigan where the prosecutor might be open to resolving in a different manner. They are very selective in the cases they might reduce down to a misdemeanor, and you really need to backup that request.

For a client, avoiding a felony conviction means everything. They can get around not driving or even going to jail, but being a felon for the rest of their life - there is no going back on that, and it cannot be expunged. It's my goal for any client charged with a DUI felony to avoid that conviction.

The proactive program is even more intense for a client with no prior or a single prior DUI offense. We might be in a situation where we are entering inpatient rehab, we are certainly testing daily for alcohol, we might even install an interlock in our own car before being ordered. It's our goal to jump on the hood and just ask for help - we want real help though - if there's a mental health issue, we try to get into a mental health court - if its related to military service, we try to get into a Veteran's Court. Sobriety court is always an option, but the prosecutor needs to agree to reduce the case, because most sobriety courts do not take felony cases.

I tell my felony DUI clients that there is no wiggle room - here is exactly what you're going to do to work with me, and it's going to get more intense as we go along. We need to make a difference in the case every single day and we earn back small pieces of credibility with the prosecutor and judge.

Below you will see my detailed thoughts on drunk driving cases from both the prosecutor viewpoint and the criminal defense side of the case.

As a former prosecutor, I had very little patience for a second offender, and most prosecutors believe the same thing, but leverage still matters. Poke holes in a prosecutor's case and well the prior offense isn't going to make the second case any stronger. If anything a prosecutor may try to come up with a compromise to make sure the defendant is at least on probation and being monitored. Those holes need to be backed up with currency outside of the courtroom so a prosecutor can justify "dismissing a DUI" when the person has a prior - that's a lot to swallow as a prosecutor and risky in the political world.

As a former prosecutor in New York City and Michigan, I had very different experiences in these roles. In New York City, defendants would typically receive quick reductions down to non-misdemeanors, with a very limited if any license suspension and rarely did a first offender receive any probation. In Michigan, drunk driving cases were handled a lot differently.

In Michigan, a drunk driving case can really vary depending upon what police department makes the arrest, because it determines what courthouse the case is heard, an who the prosecutor on the case is going to be. Some prosecutors are quick to reduce Operating While Intoxicated or Super Drunk charges down to Impaired Driving, but rarely anything below this offer. Judges typically put people on at least 12 months of probation, and some courts do send first offenders to jail.

Prosecutors typically view DUI cases as serious charges, and pretty straight forward to prosecute. Prosecutors look for evidence of driving the car then the chemical test result being over the legal limit. If they have evidence of both of those, they are confident in their case, and typically hold firm in standard offers to the defendant.

Some prosecutors have "policies" and will not make offers or will play hard ball day one, inviting a trial if you don't like the offer. The majority of prosecutors don't want to set DUI's for trial and make themselves much busier; they have large caseloads and want to resolve cases.

Most prosecutors will give some benefit of the doubt to someone with no prior DUI convictions, but will look harshly upon accidents, poor driving, an exceptionally high BAC number, and any funny business in terms of acting poorly toward the police officers. If the case is a clean traffic stop, a relatively common BAC number, there's likely to be an opening offer that might be appealing to some defendants.

As a criminal defense attorney I don't want to settle for the default/"what everyone else gets" result. I want to create more options for my client, and we do that by creating leverage both outside and inside the courtroom.

We create leverage outside of the courtroom by being proactive and changing the perception of the case from day one. When the case begins depending on your record, the prosecutor and judge will view you as a dangerous drunk driver who is lucky to not have killed someone.

As a criminal defense lawyer I anticipate the perception of my audience and look to expand the information pool with positive information about my client's past, present and future. When I say information, I don't just mean telling the prosecutor my client has a good job, a family and he's a nice guy. The information comes from real action, which begins with a substance abuse evaluation with a follow-up on recommendations.

The majority of my DUI clients are not frequent drinkers, they typically don't have more than 2-3 drinks, and have no criminal record. They have good jobs, pay their taxes, respect the law, and agree that drunk driving is not a good thing, and there should be punishment for the crime. They find themselves facing a DUI charge unexpectedly due to some variable changing on the day of the offense.

It usually stems from not planning ahead, because my client has no intention of drinking too much. The night begins without plans in place, and the environment, surroundings, people involved are different than expected, and my client drinks more than usual, and they are unfamiliar with this situation, and don't put the breaks on. The drinks keep flowing and those drinks impact positive decisions. The client's decisions are no longer completely their own and they trick themselves into believing "risking it" is a good trade off to leaving a car in a parking lot, missing an early doctors appointment or their kids little league game. They make the decision to drive, because the chances are more likely they get home ok without incident.

They fail to weigh the consequences, even if smaller and less likely - what if I get caught? Worse, what if I kill someone?

If we can make this situation make sense to a prosecutor and judge, we're going to get a lot further along in our case. Essentially we can isolate this poor choice and get away from any perception that this is typical behavior, an addiction, something we can't control. If we can pinpoint how we got there and work on that, a prosecutor and judge will view my client in a different light.

Overcoming the "dangerous drunk driver" perception starts with identifying the true issue, demonstrating that you're taking it seriously, and ready and willing to work on it. With the evaluation comes a recommendation, which is usually counseling, alcohol education, Impact Weekend, AA attendance. We do proactive community service, MADD panels and most importantly daily alcohol testing. Yes, we voluntarily begin alcohol testing, because we need to show that alcohol is not a friend, and it's not something we rely on, we're dependent on, and rather than say "I learned a lot, I don't even a want to drink", we go ahead and show it.

This is how we create leverage outside of the courtroom. I've used this leverage to turn DUI cases into non-DUI cases, probation cases into non-probation cases, and saved people's career, family and possibly their life. Prosecutor's don't like to go outside of the box, but if they do, it will require currency to justify their decision.

Being proactive outside of the courtroom is going to lead to better deals with the prosecutor, and more favorable sentences from probation and the judge, but the best outcomes also have leverage inside of the courtroom, which means we need to find something within the facts of the case to push the buttons of the prosecutor a bit - create some sort of holes or uncertainly in the case.

As a defense lawyer I view DUI cases within three windows:

1. The traffic stop
2. The arrest
3. Chemical tests

Traffic stop requires reasonable suspicion, an arrest require probable cause, and chemical tests must be done correctly to be admissible against my client. A full review of reports, videos, audio, and other evidence will hopefully provide us something to work with in terms of creating leverage. This could mean leverage for pretrial motion or at trial.

Defeating the stop could mean everything after the stop is inadmissible. Showing the arrest was not based on probable cause could suppress any field sobriety, statements, and chemical tests. Suppressing the blood or breath test could leave a prosecutor quite thin on evidence for trial.

The goal is not necessarily to file the motion or set for trial, because that runs the risk of losing control of the outcome or losing a plea offer, but having the leverage to proceed with either option - something more than a blanket "I'll set for motion or trial" - that's a bluff and prosecutors do not bite on those. You need to show them the leverage in a reasonable way - don't pull out your sword, just talk about the sword a bit.

Win with consensus, work toward a compromise that works for everyone. I've had prosecutors offer disorderly conduct and dismiss drunk driving because it was the right outcome, but I needed both the leverage within the evidence of the case, and my client needed to back it up outside of the courtroom.

CHEMICAL TESTS

As a former DUI prosecutor, I worked on 1000's of cases; the main piece of evidence was typically a chemical test, which was either a blood draw or a breath sample. In Michigan, the breath sample is collected with the Datamaster machine. Under Michigan law, the trier of fact is allowed to assume that the blood alcohol content result collected via chemical test was the same as when the driver was operating the vehicle.

As a former prosecutor my favorite lines were "over the legal limit" "more than double the legal limit" "he/she failed the test". I would push and push that chemical test being over the legal limit - what else was there to consider, the person was guilty! Anything that silly defense lawyer tells you is just smoke and mirrors - there was a test, and they failed it, end of story, find them guilty.

Many prosecutors try to over-complicate the issue and act as if they need to defend the chemical test number - the more complicated you make it, the less a jury focuses on the "failed test" concept. As a prosecutor, I did the very opposite - make it as simple as possible - juries don't want to think too much, and if you spend so much time defending something, they lose confidence in the issue and question the reliability of the evidence.

As a former prosecutor I had a different view of the blood vs breath results. In my experience, a blood test is considered to be more reliable by the "criminal law community", because well it's tested at the Michigan State Police lab, and there's supposedly less variables that can impact the result, because it is coming directly from your body. The person testifying about the result (lab tech) is also supposedly more knowledgeable and a better witness than a police officer who does the Datamaster machine.

Both prosecutors and defense lawyers tend to give the blood result more weight and if it's over the legal limit for an OWI (0.08) or Super Drunk (0.17) then there's less incentive to challenge it. I completely disagree with this perception, and bring this mindset to my criminal defense practice. Here's why:

1. In Michigan, let's say the police stop my client at 2 am. A Datamaster result would usually happen within the hour of this traffic stop, and makes for a better argument when you're telling a jury to believe the BAC level is the same as when the person was driving the car. A blood test in contrast happens hours later at the hospital, or you have to wait for someone to come to the jail to draw the blood. Typically double or triple the time goes by - a good defense lawyer will jump on that argument.

2. Once the blood is drawn, it's supposed to be sealed in a tube for testing, but that sealed tube sits around and is transported to the lab over the course of a few days. Just picture that sealed blood sample bouncing around the mail truck as it heads to Lansing in an uncontrolled environment. Throw in freezing temperatures of winter or 95 degrees in August, and that sample is compromised. The best is when the lab tech brags about the sample being stored in a controlled environment prior to testing (but after bouncing around the mail truck in 95 degree weather for 3 days) - all I have to say is REASONABLE DOUBT.

3. It's a pain to get the lab tech to come to court to testify and

limits your flexibility to set the case for trial. It's so much easier to have the police officer available to come in and testify.

Sure a Datamaster has it's faults, but cops are trained not to know enough to be challenged. They have a procedure and if they follow it, that's it. They are not required to know how the machine works or why it does X, Y and Z but rather to follow steps. If the jury likes the cop and they believe he followed the steps then they will probably buy into the result and not find reasonable doubt. There's also usually two tests (not required), but the second result can confirm the first result vs a single blood test result.

As a criminal defense lawyer, I find that prosecutors are more confident in the blood draw, but at trial those are easier to challenge. And the goal is not to show the test is wrong, faulty or an error, but rather just raise enough doubt to get a not-guilty verdict, and the door is wide open on the blood test.

With the Datamaster, I am looking for numbers close to the limits of 0.08 and 0.17 as there are built in margins of error listed in the training manual for the operator. I am also looking for a police officer who is going to be chatty and give me open windows. Officers are trained not to discuss how the machine works or WHAT IF's but human nature makes most officers answer questions and be open to possibilities. If the officer answers YES IT'S POSSIBLE to enough questions then that's my reasonable doubt. After all it's a machine and the person pressing the buttons doesn't know how it works, why should be believe the result?

FIELD SOBRIETY TESTS

As a former prosecutor I used to think field sobriety tests were a golden ticket to conviction. Along with the chemical tests, I had my police officer administering a number of super reliable tests and the results were typically favorable to prosecution. I would look at the police report and boom, boom, boom, I had the defendant sinking his/her own case. It wasn't until a few skilled defense lawyers began taking apart these tests that I soon realized they were not as reliable as I once thought.

In Michigan a witness, typically a police officer is allowed to testify to Standardized Field Sobriety Tests (SFST) results and how they relate to impairment if the witness is qualified by knowledge, skill, experience, training, or education. The law specifically states that the Horizontal Gaze Nystagmus (HGN) is admissible under this provision by an officer trained in how to perform the test.

In Michigan "Standardized Field Sobriety Test" means one of the standardized tests validated by the National Highway Traffic Safety Administration (NHTSA). A field sobriety test is considered a SFST under this section if it is administered in substantial compliance with the standards prescribed by NHTSA.

In simple terms if the police officer is qualified and follows the rules then the evidence can be introduced to the trier of fact or at a evidence hearing. The problem for many people charged is their attorney simply reads the police report; they don't look into if these tests were done correctly. A cop is NOT going to say they did them wrong in the report - it takes watching the video and listening to the instructions to confirm compliance.

Based on my experience as a prosecutor, I know that the prosecutor has not watched the video or firmed up these tests; they just assume they are done correctly. This means if I look further into the issue and spot problems, they WILL NOT be prepared to respond at a hearing or trial, and I have a good shot at making a statement in front of a jury or judge and hopefully discredit these tests.

According to a State of Michigan law enforcement memo, the SFSTs are designed as divided attention or psychophysical tests which involve requiring the subject to concentrate on both mental and physical tasks at the same time.

These tests are designed to mimic the different abilities and tasks involved in operating a motor vehicle. These include information processing, short-term memory, judgment and decision making, balance, steady and sure reactions, clear vision, small muscle control and coordination of limbs.

As a criminal attorney, I am only looking for the BIG THREE: HGN, Walk & Turn and One Leg Stand, because any other test is not standardized and a fiction of the officer's imagination. An officer can just as easily as my client to recite the Detroit Tigers lineup as he can the alphabet - I am going to discredit anything outside of the BIG THREE right away.

According to various studies, the HGN is only 77 percent accurate, the Walk and Turn is 68 percent accurate and the One Leg Stand is only 65 percent accurate.

As a prosecutor, I would quickly glance at the officer's narrative and just assume "LOOKS GOOD" and move on. As a criminal defense lawyer, I dig into the details and test the officer narrative to the video/audio. Even a small difference between report and video could mean putting the officer in a position of trying to make his report/narrative more favorable and really discredit the whole process. We get the benefit of the doubt on the things we can't see and hear if what we can see and hear is not 100 percent accurate, and it's so important to make a big stink about it, because a jury doesn't know any better.

The first test is always the most fishy - the HGN, because there is no video or audio of what the officer is actually observing on my client since it's his eyes - I am looking for proper or improper instructions and if I can see how the officer is actually administering the tests. If he does it by the book, I am hoping that his credibility is put into question on another test, which I can see better such as the one leg stand or walk & turn, so I can argue that it simply taints all the tests.

According to the officer training manual here are the proper instructions:

1)Please remove your glasses (if worn).
2)Put your feet together, hands at your side. Keep your head still and follow this stimulus with your eyes only.
3)Keep looking at the stimulus until the test is over.
4)Do not move your head.
5)Do you understand the instructions?

The officer will then position the stimulus 12-15 inches from the suspect's nose and slightly above eye level. He or she will first check to see if both pupils are equal in size (if they aren't, this may indicate a head injury). The officer will then make sure the eyes are able to track together (called equal tracking) across the suspect's entire field of vision.

Here the officer is looking to see if the eyes track the stimulus together or if one eye lags behind the other (this would indicate medical disorder, injury or blindness). After this is done, the officer continues with the test as listed below:

The officer is now looking for the three clues in each eye, so 6 total clues.

1) The Lack of Smooth Pursuit –the eyes can be observed to jerk or bounce as they follow a smoothly moving stimulus, such as a finger or penlight. The eyes of an unimpaired person will follow smoothly, i.e., a windshield wiper gliding across a wet windshield; whereas the eyes of an impaired person will follow in a jerking manner, i.e., a windshield wiper moving across a dry windshield.

a.Instruct the subject to hold their head still and to follow the stimulus with their eyes only.
b.Move the stimulus smoothly, all the way to the subject's left, then all the way to the right, then back again all the way to the left, then once again all the way back to the right.
c.While the eye is moving, examine it for evidence of a lack of smooth pursuit.
d.Each eye counts as one clue for scoring purposes.

2) Distinct and Sustained Nystagmus at Maximum Deviation – distinct and sustained nystagmus is observed when the eye is held at maximum deviation for a minimum of four seconds. People's eyes exhibit a slight jerking at maximum deviation even when unimpaired, but this jerking will not last more than

a few seconds. In alcohol-impaired individuals, the jerking is larger, more pronounced, sustained for more than four seconds, and easily observable. Nystagmus at maximum deviation is observed when the eye is moved to the point where there is no longer any white left in the side of the eye. The nystagmus can be observed to act in a back and forth "popping" motion.

a.Position the stimulus as before.
b.Move the stimulus all the way to the subject's left side and hold it there so that the subject's eye is turned as far to the side as possible.
c.Hold the eye at that position for a minimum of 4 seconds to check carefully for any jerking that may be present.
d.Then move the stimulus all the way to the subject's right side and hold it there for a minimum of 4 seconds checking again for any jerking that may be present.
e.Repeat both steps b and d (check each eye twice).
f.A definite, strong jerking must be seen; a slightly or barely visible tremor is not sufficient enough to count as a clue.
g.Each eye counts as one clue for scoring purposes.

3) Onset of Nystagmus Prior to 45 Degrees –the point at which the officer first observes nystagmus or jerkingin the eye. If the jerking begins prior to 45 degrees (typically when the stimulus is aligned with the subject's shoulder),recent studies have shown that the jerking corresponds with a 0.08-plus BAC. The higher the degree of impairment, the sooner the nystagmus will be observable.

a.Position the stimulus as before.
b.Slowly move the stimulus to the subject's left side, carefully watching the eye for the first sign of jerking. c.When you think

that you see the eye jerk, stop moving the stimulus and hold it still.

d.Make sure to verify that the eye is in fact jerking.

e.Once you have established that you have located the point of onset, estimate the angle.

f.Repeat this procedure on the subject's right eye.

g.Repeat both steps b and f (check each eye twice).h.Each eye counts as one clue for scoring purposes.

Next up is the Walk and Turn - officer is looking for 8 clues. Here are the instructions, which I am looking for compliance or non-compliance.

1)Put your left foot on the line, then your right foot on the line ahead of your left. Keep your arms at your side. (Demonstrate)

2)Do not start until I tell you to do so.

3)Do you understand? (Officer must receive an affirmative response)

4)When I tell you to begin, take heel-to-toe steps on the line. (Demonstrate) To turn around, keep one foot on the line and return nine steps.

5)When you turn on the ninth step, keep your front foot on the line and turn taking several small steps with the other foot. (Demonstrate) Take heel-to-toe steps back down the line.

6)Keep your arms at your side at all times, watch your feet, and count each step out loud. Once walking begins, do not stop until you've completed the test.

7)Do you understand the instructions?

8)You may begin.

9)If suspect doesn't understand some part of the instructions, officer should repeat only that part which suspect does not understand.

Here are the 8 clues the officer is looking for during the test.

1)Can't balance during instructions
2)Starts too soon Walking Stage clues:
3)Stops while walking
4)Doesn't touch heel-to-toe
5)Steps off line
6)Uses arms for balance
7)Loses balance on turn or turns incorrectly
8)Takes the wrong number of steps

Officer will be quick to point out which clues he observed, but it's important to point out what he didn't observe. Let's say the officer lists 3-4 of them, well that means you didn't see the other 4-5, which means something.

Finally, we have the one-leg-stand - here are the proper instructions:

1)Stand with your feet together and your arms at your side. (Demonstrate)
2)Maintain position until told otherwise.
3)When I tell you to, I want you to raise one leg (either leg) approximately six inches off the ground, foot pointed out, both legs straight, and look at the elevated foot. Count out loud in the following manner: 1001, 1002, 1003, and so on, until told to stop.
4)Do you understand the instructions?
5)You may begin the test.

The timing is very critical during this test. The original research has shown that many impaired subjects are able to stand on one leg for up to 25 seconds but that few can do so for 30 seconds or more.

The One-Leg-Stand is divided into two phases:

1) Instruction Stage and 2) Balance and Counting Stage.

During the Instruction Stage, the subject must stand with their feet together, keep their arms at their sides, and listen to the instructions.

During the Balance and Counting Stage, the subject must perform and complete the exercise as instructed.

There are 4 clues that an officer is looking for during the OLS exercise.

They are as follows:

1)Sways while balancing
2)Uses arms for balance
3)Hops
4)Puts foot down

Same as the walk and turn, if the officer points out clues he observed, it is important to point out what he didn't see.

These field sobriety tests are so ripe for attack by a defense attorney, but it takes some extra work. Field sobriety test issues can be used to challenge an arrest or can be used to help argue a close call BAC case. A chemical test result can be presumed to be what the driver would have registered while driving, but that assumption is not required. If I have a 0.09 BAC an hour later, but the field sobriety tests are actually pretty good, I can argue the deviation, plus timing, plus rising blood that my client wasn't above the limit while driving. I can also use the field sobriety tests to challenge an arrest, especially if there is no PBT result over the limit.

The possibilities are endless, you just need to be prepared to look deeper into the issue.

IMPLIED CONSENT

As a former prosecutor, I had no formal participation in an implied consent issue.

According to the Michigan Secretary of State:

"If arrested for drunk driving in Michigan, you will be required to take a chemical test to determine your bodily alcohol content (BAC). Under Michigan's Implied Consent Law, all drivers are considered to have given their consent to this test. If you refuse a test, six points will be added to your driver record and your license, or non-resident operating privilege, will be suspended for one year. A suspension of a license, or non-resident operating privilege, is automatic for any refusal to submit to the test. This is a separate consequence from any subsequent convictions resulting from the traffic stop. If you are arrested a second time in seven years and again unreasonably refuse the test, six points will be added to your driver record and your license, or non-resident operating privilege, will be suspended for two years. If you refuse to take the test under the Implied Consent Law or if the test shows your BAC is 0.08 or more, your Michigan driver's license will be destroyed by the officer and you will be issued a 625g paper permit to drive until your case is resolved in court.

The Implied Consent suspension may be appealed to the Administrative Hearings Section. The request for hearing must be mailed within 14 days of the date of arrest or your operator's or chauffeur's license and vehicle group designation or operating privilege will be automatically suspended. You are not required to have an attorney at this hearing, but an attorney may represent you if you wish"

As you can see, the county, city, township or municipality prosecutor has nothing to do with this potential action on your license as it is not criminal and has no correlation to the outcome in the courtroom. Most defense lawyers stop here and take the prosecutor out of the case and try to go toe to toe with the police officer at the hearing. As a former prosecutor I barely even knew what the implied consent law was, because no defense lawyer brought it to my attention.

As a criminal attorney who is always looking for options for my clients, I focus on this line, which is also listed on the Michigan Secretary of State website

"Please note - A request by a law enforcement officer or prosecutor to withdraw a report of refusal must be received by the Department no later than the date of hearing."

This means that the police officer or the prosecutor can withdraw the refusal, meaning there is no need to hold the hearing and risk loss of license for a full year and six points on the driving record. Most prosecutors have never even heard of this power they have, and most would be too afraid to use it if not approached in the correct way. Same holds true for the police officers; if taken by surprise, they are unlikely to OVERTURN something in fear of getting in trouble or "being tricked".

This is a delicate subject to bring up to a prosecutor, and must be done in the right way. Outright seeking this outcome is usually turned down because the prosecutor isn't comfortable as they feel like they are trying to be fleeced or tricked into agreeing. I use the proactive items that my client has already achieved and continues to work on as I play the common sense/moral card. My client is working his/her butt off without being required to do so, and if we're going to be resolving the case together there is going to be some sort of license suspension, supervision of my client; why do we need to take the license away for a full year too?

In my experience once a prosecutor fully understands their unique and mostly unknown power, and my client's proactive accomplishments are brought to light, it just makes sense to work with us on mitigating the implied consent implications and coming to a mutual resolution of all issues. If we can bring the prosecutor into the implied consent case, we can come up with a universal outcome rather than treating the two issues as separate issues where you lose the ability to make a great overall deal for the client.

You win the implied consent issue by empowering and respecting the prosecutor.

SOBRIETY COURTS

As a former prosecutor my main goal was to prosecute the case; marching orders were to charge and convict; the defendant was a name and a charge with no backstory. It was up to the criminal defense attorney to provide additional information for consideration, but this rarely happened. If someone plead guilty to drunk driving, I would move onto the next case unless there was something unique to address at sentencing.

In Michigan, if convicted of a second drunk driving offense within 7 years, the defendant loses his/her ability to drive for a full year, there is also a mandatory five days jail with most judges sentencing to more than those five days. One possibility to work around some of those sanctions is by entering a sobriety court.

Not all courts have a sobriety court, and different courts have different qualifications to enter the court. The State of Michigan must certify that court in order for the possibility of receiving a hardship license - there are some courts that call themselves a sobriety court, but they are not certified by the State of Michigan.

As a former prosecutor I would have no issue with a defendant entering sobriety court as it was an indication that the person was taking responsibility for their actions and seeking help. Sure they are probably motivated by potentially receiving a license and maybe avoiding jail, but I left that up to the judge, and they would be required to have an ignition interlock on their car to receive this hardship license.

Depending on the court, it may be a very straight forward process - if you offend and live in the same jurisdiction and there's a sobriety court then great you're probably going to get into the sobriety court. What happens when the court you offend in does not have a sobriety court, or they do have a court, but they say you must also live there in order to gain the benefit of the court? Well you can move, but is that realistic? Probably not.

This is where its necessary to step outside of the box and earn a special outcome. If the court itself is not willing to take you into their sobriety court or they don't have one, it's time to go shopping for another sobriety court. Now, why would some other court take you? That doesn't make a lot of sense, and that is exactly why we're proactive from day one and demonstrating the proper commitment, work ethic and mindset to be an excellent candidate for entry. There's going to be a sobriety court out there who appreciates the work product and will consider your entry into their court, if not only because you will be an excellent example - a superstar for others to aspire to, and an example to point to for the judge.

Sobriety court is no different than a sports team. The judge is the coach or manager and he has his players (the sobriety court participants). Everyone knows what everyone is up to and individual performance impacts the team has a whole and their teammates. If most are not complying or following the rules then it sets a bad example for others, but if it's the opposite, you're going to inspire the other teammates to go the extra mile. When the safety of the roads of Michigan and the population as a whole are depending on the sobriety court to help people no re-offend, having a good environment is extremely important.

I am proud that many of my clients have been accepted into other sobriety courts as a transfer case due to their proactive steps and impressive track record. They went from losing their license and mandatory jail to having a license and the jail being suspended due to entry into the sobriety court, because of their hard work.

HARDSHIP LICENSE

As a former prosecutor I worked on 1000's of drunk driving cases, and one of the main concerns of the person charges was their ability to drive. A person doesn't realize how important the ability to drive actually is until they are no longer able to do so. It means you can't drive to work, school, drive your kids or family around, go grocery shopping, leave the house to eat or entertainment. Losing your license can be a huge burden on a spouse or friends and family, and I have seen relationships ruined because someone can't drive their car.

One role that a prosecutor has in Michigan is on a circuit court hardship appeal. If someone violates the implied consent law for refusing a chemical test and that ruling is upheld on appeal, a petitioner (the defendant) has the option to file a hardship appeal with the circuit court on the basis of hardship if this is there first implied consent issue. Some counties will have a representative from the Attorney General's Office as a representative for the Michigan Secretary of State, while others will actually have the county prosecutor act as the representative.

The court is ultimately looking for a real hardship tied into your ability to work, go to school, perform obligations of your probation and other listed issues. They also want to be sure that public transportation or reasonable alternative accommodations are not available to the petitioner. If you lived down the block from where you work, you could not claim a legitimate hardship to get to and from work as a basis of receiving the license.

Many people walk into court and simply say "here is where I

work, and here is where I live, I need to drive". That is lazy and not the most effective way to convince both a judge and prosecutor to OVERTURN a license suspension. Think about what that means - you violated the law (implied consent law), your license was suspended because of it, and now you're asking for that decision to be overturned, and all you're going to do is show where you work and where you live?

As a former prosecutor I witnessed too many of these situations go wrong, because people did not over-prepare and take the process as seriously as they should from day one. As a proactive criminal defense attorney, we may be shifting gears from our criminal case to the circuit court, but we can use all of our proactive accomplishments for these stage as well.

The most important parts will be the substance abuse evaluation and any subsequent following of that recommendation along with the daily alcohol testing. Neither is required, but the substance abuse evaluation is expected, and daily alcohol testing is usually the cherry on top of receiving the hardship license.

I can't tell you how many times I've been out in the hallway with the prosecutor/AG representative with another attorney, and all they have is "well it's his first implied consent, and he works 20 miles from where he lives" - I sometimes wish I was the prosecutor again so I could tell that defense attorney - "well he shouldn't have refused the chemical test, I'm not changing the suspension for you" - that's just lazy lawyering - the client could have done the same thing in court.

I have my substance abuse evaluation ready, AA meeting logs, alcohol insight class completion certificate, counseling letters and printout of our daily alcohol testing. We're showing the prosecutor that from day one we were open about learning from the situation, followed the recommendation of the health care professional, and you should grant this hardship, because my client HAS NOT BEEN DRINKING and here is proof of that. Not all petitioners are being alcohol tested or even on probation with a court so there's concerns about handing someone a license who is actively drinking - what better than to show proof that my client is not drinking?

I always believe in building consensus with a prosecutor, because I learned if you want to go toe to toe with a prosecutor, they will prevail more than they are defeated, because a judge is naturally more familiar with that person and it's the more conservative thing to do. Handing my client the ability to drive soon after a DUI incident is risky, and I acknowledge that - that is why my clients work their butts off to show they should be granted the opportunity to earn back the trust of the prosecutor, judge and community.

If I can get the prosecutor to sign a stipulated order for a hardship license in the hallway and we can walk into the courtroom and BOTH tell the judge we want petitioner to receive a hardship license, what's the judge going to do? Say no? Probably not. Some judges will still have concerns, especially newer judges or judges who are not that familiar with these type of proceedings, but I use the same proactive tools with the judge to get my client over the hump, and get them back on the road.

MICHIGAN TRIAL COURT DIRECTORY

The following court directory and judicial listings are the most frequent counties where we help clients with legal issues. We do travel outside of the listed counties. Feel free to contact our office for additional information on a county not listed.

WAYNE COUNTY
3rd Circuit Court

Frank Murphy Hall of Justice

Detroit, MI 48226

(313) 224-5261

Honorable Robert J. Colombo, Jr., Chief Judge

Honorable David J. Allen, Circuit Judge

Honorable Mariam Bazzi, Circuit Judge

Honorable Annette J. Berry, Circuit Judge

Honorable Gregory D. Bill, Circuit Judge

Honorable Ulysses W. Boykin, Circuit Judge

Honorable Karen Y. Braxton, Circuit Judge

Honorable Megan Maher Brennan, Circuit Judge

Ms. Zenell Brown, Court Administrator

Honorable Thomas Cameron, Circuit Judge

Honorable Jerome C. Cavanagh, Circuit Judge

Honorable Eric William Cholack, Circuit Judge

Honorable James R. Chylinski, Circuit Judge

Honorable Kevin J. Cox, Circuit Judge

Honorable Melissa Anne Cox, Circuit Judge

Honorable Paul John Cusick, Circuit Judge

Honorable Christopher D. Dingell, Circuit Judge

Honorable Charlene M. Elder, Circuit Judge

Honorable Vonda R. Evans, Circuit Judge

Honorable Wanda Evans, Circuit Judge

Honorable Edward Ewell, Jr., Circuit Judge

Honorable Patricia Susan Fresard, Circuit Judge

Honorable Sheila Ann Gibson, Circuit Judge

Honorable John H. Gillis, Jr., Circuit Judge

Honorable Alexis Glendening, Circuit Judge

Honorable David Alan Groner, Circuit Judge

Honorable Richard B. Halloran, Circuit Judge

Honorable Adel A. Harb, Circuit Judge

Honorable Cynthia Gray Hathaway, Circuit Judge

Honorable Dana Margaret Hathaway, Circuit Judge

Honorable Daniel Arthur Hathaway, Circuit Judge

Honorable Thomas M. J. Hathaway, Circuit Judge

Honorable Charles S. Hegarty, Circuit Judge

Honorable Catherine Heise, Circuit Judge

Honorable Susan L. Hubbard, Circuit Judge

Honorable Muriel D. Hughes, Circuit Judge

Honorable Edward Joseph, Circuit Judge

Honorable Connie Marie Kelley, Circuit Judge

Honorable Timothy Michael Kenny, Circuit Judge

Honorable Qiana D. Lillard, Circuit Judge

Honorable Kathleen M. McCarthy, Circuit Judge

Honorable Bruce U. Morrow, Circuit Judge

Honorable John A. Murphy, Circuit Judge

Honorable Lynne A. Pierce, Circuit Judge

Honorable Lita Masini Popke, Circuit Judge

Honorable Kelly Ramsey, Circuit Judge

Honorable Richard M. Skutt, Circuit Judge

Honorable Mark T. Slavens, Circuit Judge

Honorable Leslie Kim Smith, Circuit Judge

Honorable Virgil C. Smith, Circuit Judge

Honorable Martha M. Snow, Circuit Judge

Honorable Craig S. Strong, Circuit Judge

Honorable Brian R. Sullivan, Circuit Judge

Honorable Lawrence S. Talon, Circuit Judge

Honorable Deborah A. Thomas, Circuit Judge

Honorable Margaret M. Van Houten, Circuit Judge

Honorable Shannon N. Walker, Circuit Judge

16th District Court (Livonia)

32765 Five Mile Rd.

Livonia, MI 48154

(734) 466-2500

Honorable Sean P. Kavanagh, Chief Judge

Honorable Kathleen J. McCann, District Judge

Ms. Natalie Stojcevska, Court Administrator

17th District Court (Redford)

15111 Beech-Daly Rd.

Redford, MI 48239

(313) 387-2790

Honorable Karen Khalil, Chief Judge

Mr. Matthew Sawicki, Court Administrator

Honorable Charlotte L. Wirth, District Judge

18th District Court (Westland)

36675 Ford Rd.

Westland, MI 48185

(734) 595-8720

Honorable Sandra A. Cicirelli, Chief Judge

Mr. James Gibbs, Court Administrator

Honorable Mark A. McConnell, District Judge

19th District Court (Dearborn)

16077 Michigan Ave.

Dearborn, MI 48126

(313) 943-2060

Honorable Sam A. Salamey, Chief Judge

Mr. Eric F. Cyman, Court Administrator

Honorable L. Eugene Hunt, Jr., District Judge

Honorable Mark W. Somers, District Judge

20th District Court (Dearborn Heights)

25637 Michigan Ave.

Dearborn Heights, MI 48125

(313) 277-7480

Honorable Mark J. Plawecki, Chief Judge

Ms. Michelle Adkins, Court Administrator

Honorable David Turfe, District Judge

21st District Court (Garden City)

6000 N. Middlebelt Rd.

Garden City, MI 48135

(734) 793-1680

Honorable Richard L. Hammer, Jr., Chief Judge

Ms. Kristin Remer, Court Administrator

22nd District Court (Inkster)

26279 Michigan Ave.

Inkster, MI 48141

(313) 277-8200

Honorable Sabrina L. Johnson, Chief Judge

Ms. Priscilla Gibbs, Court Administrator

23rd District Court (Taylor)

23365 Goddard

Taylor, MI 48180

(734) 374-1334

Honorable Geno Salomone, Chief Judge

Honorable Joseph D. Slaven, District Judge

Ms. Deanna Warunek, Court Administrator

24th District Court (Allen Park)

6515 Roosevelt Rd.

Allen Park, MI 48101

(313) 928-0535

Honorable John T. Courtright, Chief Judge Ms. Dawn Grubbs,

Court Administrator

Honorable Richard A. Page, District Judge

25th District Court (Lincoln Park)

1475 Cleophus

Lincoln Park, MI 48146

(313) 382-8603

Honorable Gregory A. Clifton, Chief Judge

Ms. Teri Michael, Court Administrator

Honorable David J. Zelenak, District Judge

27th District Court (Wyandotte)

2015 Biddle Ave.

Wyandotte, MI 48192

(734) 324-4475

Honorable Randy L. Kalmbach, Chief Judge

28th District Court (Southgate)

14720 Reaume Parkway

Southgate, MI 48195

(734) 258-3068

Honorable James A. Kandrevas, Chief Judge

29th District Court (Wayne)

34808 Sims Ave.

Wayne, MI 48184

(734) 722-5220

Honorable Laura Redmond Mack, Chief Judge

30th District Court (Highland Park)

12050 Woodward Ave.

Highland Park, MI 48203

(313) 252-0300

Honorable Brigette R. Officer-Hill, Chief Judge

31st District Court (Hamtramck)

3401 Evaline Ave.

Hamtramck, MI 48212

(313) 800-5248

Honorable Alexis G Krot, Chief Judge

32A District Court (Harper Woods)

19617 Harper Ave.

Harper Woods, MI 48225

Honorable Daniel S. Palmer, Chief Judge

33rd District Court (Woodhaven)

19000 Van Horn

Woodhaven, MI 48183

(734) 671-0201

Honorable Jennifer Coleman Hesson, Chief Judge

Honorable James Kurt Kersten, District Judge

Honorable Michael K. McNally, District Judge

Ms. Amy Zawacki, Court Administrator

34th District Court (Romulus)

11131 Wayne Rd.

Romulus, MI 48174

(734) 941-4462

Honorable Tina Brooks Green, Chief Judge

Mr. Alan Hindman, Court Administrator

Honorable Brian A. Oakley, District Judge

Honorable David M. Parrott, District Judge

35th District Court (Plymouth)

---

660 Plymouth Rd.

Plymouth, MI 48170

(734) 459-4740

Magistrate Frank Whren

Honorable Michael J. Gerou, Chief Judge

Ms. Pam Avdoulos, Court Administrator

Honorable Ronald W. Lowe, District Judge

Honorable James A. Plakas, District Judge

36th District Court (Detroit)

---

421 Madison Ave.

Detroit, MI 48226

(313) 965-2200

Honorable Nancy McCaughan Blount, Chief Judge

Honorable Lydia Nance Adams, District Judge

Honorable Roberta C. Archer, District Judge

Honorable Christopher Michael Blount, District Judge

Honorable Izetta F. Bright, District Judge

Honorable Demetria Brue, District Judge

Honorable Esther Lynise Bryant-Weekes, District Judge

Honorable Donald Coleman, District Judge

Honorable Kahlilia Yvette Davis, District Judge

Honorable Prentis Edwards, Jr., District Judge

Honorable Deborah Geraldine Ford, District Judge

Honorable Austin William Garrett, District Judge

Honorable Ruth Ann Garrett, District Judge

Honorable Ronald Giles, District Judge

Honorable Adrienne Hinnant-Johnson, District Judge

Honorable Shannon A. Holmes, District Judge

Honorable Patricia L. Jefferson, District Judge

Honorable Kenyetta Stanford Jones, District Judge

Honorable Alicia A. Jones-Coleman, District Judge

Honorable Kenneth J. King, District Judge

Honorable Deborah L. Langston, District Judge

Honorable William McConico, District Judge

Honorable Donna R. Milhouse, District Judge

Honorable B. Pennie Millender, District Judge

Honorable Cylenthia LaToye Miller, District Judge

Ms. Kelli Moore Owen, Court Administrator

Honorable David Perkins, District Judge

Honorable Kevin F. Robbins, District Judge

Honorable David S. Robinson, Jr., District Judge

Honorable Michael E. Wagner, District Judge

Honorable Larry D. Williams, Jr., District Judge

Grosse Pte. Municipal Court (Grosse Pointe City)

17147 Maumee

Grosse Pointe, MI 48230

(313) 343-5262

Honorable Russell F. Ethridge, Chief Judge

Ms. Kim Silvestro, Court Administrator

Grosse Pte. Farms Municipal Court (Grosse Pointe Farms)

---

90 Kerby Rd.

Grosse Pte. Farms, MI 48236

(313) 885-2104

Honorable Matthew R. Rumora, Chief Judge

Ms. Madeline Eberhardt, Court Administrator

Grosse Pte. Park Municipal Court

15115 E. Jefferson Ave.

Grosse Pte. Park, MI 48230

(313) 822-3535

Honorable Carl F. Jarboe, Chief Judge

Ms. Susan Thomas, Court Administrator

Grosse Pte. Woods Municipal Court

(Grosse Pointe Woods)

20025 Mack Plaza Drive

Grosse Pte. Woods, MI 48236

(313) 343-2455

Honorable Theodore A. Metry, Chief Judge Ms.

Susan Tobin, Court Administrator

OAKLAND COUNTY
6th Circuit Court

Courthouse Tower

1200 N. Telegraph Rd.

Pontiac, MI 48341

(248) 858-0345

Honorable Nanci J. Grant, Chief Judge

Honorable James M. Alexander, Circuit Judge

Honorable Martha Anderson, Circuit Judge

Honorable Leo Bowman, Circuit Judge

Honorable Mary Ellen Brennan, Circuit Judge

Honorable Rae Lee Chabot, Circuit Judge

Honorable Lisa Ortlieb Gorcyca, Circuit Judge

Honorable Hala Y. Jarbou, Circuit Judge

Honorable Shalina D. Kumar, Circuit Judge

Honorable Denise Langford-Morris, Circuit Judge

Honorable Lisa Langton, Circuit Judge

Honorable Jeffery S. Matis, Circuit Judge

Honorable Cheryl A. Matthews, Circuit Judge

Honorable Karen D. McDonald, Circuit Judge

Honorable Phyllis C. McMillen, Circuit Judge

Honorable Daniel Patrick O'Brien, Circuit Judge

Honorable Wendy Lynn Potts, Circuit Judge

Honorable Victoria Ann Valentine, Circuit Judge

Honorable Michael D. Warren, Jr., Circuit Judge

Mr. Kevin Oeffner, Court Administrator

43rd District Court (Hazel Park)

---

43 E. Nine Mile Rd.

Hazel Park, MI 48030

(248) 547-3034

Honorable Joseph Longo, Chief Judge

Honorable Charles G. Goedert, District Judge

Honorable Keith P. Hunt, District Judge

Ms. Diana M. Nimmoor, Court Administrator

43rd District Court (Ferndale)

---

305 E. Nine Mile Rd.

Ferndale, MI 48220

(248) 547-8700

Honorable Joseph Longo, Chief Judge

Honorable Charles G. Goedert, District Judge

Honorable Keith P. Hunt, District Judge

Ms. Linda S. Carroll, Court Administrator

43rd District Court (Madison Heights)

---

200 W. Thirteen Mile Rd.

Madison Heights, MI 48071

(248) 583-1800

Honorable Joseph Longo, Chief Judge

Honorable Charles G. Goedert, District Judge

Honorable Keith P. Hunt, District Judge

44th District Court (Royal Oak)

PO Box 20

400 E. 11 Mile Road

Royal Oak, MI 48068

(248) 246-3600

Honorable Derek W. Meinecke, Chief Judge

Honorable James L. Wittenberg, District Judge

Mr. Gary W. Dodge, Court Administrator

45th District Court (Oak Park)

13600 Oak Park Blvd.

Oak Park, MI 48237

(248) 691-7433

Honorable Michelle Friedman Appel, Chief Judge

Honorable David M. Gubow, District Judge

Ms. Nancy Waldmann, Court Administrator

46th District Court (Southfield)

PO Box 2055

26000 Evergreen Rd.

Southfield, MI 48076

(248) 796-5800

Honorable Shelia R. Johnson, Chief Judge

Honorable Cynthia Arvant, District Judge

Honorable Debra Nance, District Judge

Ms. Renee R. Shelide, Court Administrator

47th District Court (Farmington Hills)

31605 W. Eleven Mile Road

Farmington Hills, MI 48336

(248) 871-2900

Honorable James Brady, Chief Judge

Honorable Marla E. Parker, District Judge

Mr. David L. Walsh, Court Administrator

48th District Court (Bloomfield Hills)

PO Box 3200

4280 Telegraph Rd.

Bloomfield Hills, MI 48302

(248) 647-1141

Honorable Marc Barron, Chief Judge

Honorable Diane D'Agostini, District Judge

Honorable Kimberly Small, District Judge

Mr. Jim VerPloeg, Court Administrator

50th District Court (Pontiac)

---

70 N. Saginaw

Pontiac, MI 48342

(248) 758-3800

Honorable Cynthia Thomas Walker, Chief Judge

Honorable Ronda Fowlkes Gross, District Judge

Honorable Michael C. Martinez, District Judge

Honorable Preston G. Thomas, District Judge

Ms. Lynette Ward, Court Administrator

51st District Court (Waterford)

5100 Civic Center Drive

Waterford, MI 48329

(248) 674-4655

Honorable Richard D. Kuhn, Jr., Chief Judge

Honorable Todd A. Fox, District Judge

52nd District Court – (Novi)

48150 Grand River Ave.

Novi, MI 48374

(248) 305-6080

Honorable Julie A. Nicholson, Chief Judge

Honorable Robert Bondy, District Judge

Honorable Thomas David Law, District Judge

Honorable Travis Reeds, District Judge

52nd District Court (Clarkston)

5850 Lorac

Clarkston, MI 48346

(248) 625-4888

Honorable Julie A. Nicholson, Chief Judge

Honorable Joseph G. Fabrizio, District Judge

Honorable Kelley Renae Kostin, District Judge

Ms. Sharon Rupe, Court Administrator

52nd District Court (Rochester Hills)

---

700 Barclay Circle

Rochester Hills, MI 48307

(248) 853-5553

Honorable Julie A. Nicholson, Chief Judge

Honorable Lisa L. Asadoorian, District Judge

Honorable Nancy Tolwin Carniak, District Judge

Mr. Brian Matthew Henderson, Court Administrator

52nd District Court (Troy)

---

520 W. Big Beaver Road

Troy, MI 48084

(248) 528-0400

Honorable Julie A. Nicholson, Chief Judge

Honorable Kirsten Nielsen Hartig, District Judge

Honorable Maureen M. McGinnis, District Judge

Ms. B. Jill Palulian, Court Administrator

MACOMB COUNTY
16th Circuit Court (Macomb)

Macomb County Court Building

40 N. Main

Mt. Clemens, MI 48043

(586) 469-5150

Honorable James M. Biernat, Jr., Chief Judge

Ms. Julie Bovenschen, Court Administrator

Honorable Richard L. Caretti, Circuit Judge

Honorable Diane M. Druzinski, Circuit Judge

Honorable Jennifer Faunce, Circuit Judge

Honorable James M. Maceroni, Circuit Judge

Honorable Carl J. Marlinga, Circuit Judge

Honorable Racheal Rancilio, Circuit Judge

Honorable Edward A. Servitto, Jr., Circuit Judge

Honorable Michael E. Servitto, Circuit Judge

Honorable Mark S. Switalski, Circuit Judge

Honorable Matthew S. Switalski, Circuit Judge

Honorable Joseph Toia, Circuit Judge

Honorable Kathryn A. Viviano, Circuit Judge

Honorable Tracey A. Yokich, Circuit Judge

37th District Court (Center Line)

7070 E. Ten Mile Rd.

Center Line, MI 48015

(586) 757-8333

Honorable John M. Chmura, Chief Judge

Honorable Michael Chupa, District Judge

Honorable Suzanne M Faunce, District Judge

Honorable Matthew P. Sabaugh, District Judge

37th District Court (Warren)

Edward A. Rea Judicial Bldg.

8300 Common Rd.

Warren, MI 48093

(586) 574-4900

Honorable John M. Chmura, Chief Judge

Honorable Michael Chupa, District Judge

Honorable Suzanne M Faunce, District Judge

Honorable Matthew P. Sabaugh, District Judge

Mr. Robert Curtis, Court Administrator

38th District Court (Eastpointe)

16101 Nine Mile Rd.

Eastpointe, MI 48021

(586) 445-5020

Honorable Carl F. Gerds, III, Chief Judge

Ms. Karen Haydett, Court Administrator

39th District Court (Roseville)

29733 Gratiot Ave.

Roseville, MI 48066

(586) 773-2010

Honorable Marco A. Santia, Chief Judge

Honorable Joseph F. Boedeker, District Judge

Honorable Catherine B. Steenland, District Judge

39th District Court (Fraser)

PO Box 10

City Hall

33000 Garfield Rd.

Fraser, MI 48026

(586) 293-3137

Honorable Marco A. Santia, Chief Judge

Honorable Joseph F. Boedeker, District Judge

Honorable Catherine B. Steenland, District Judge

40th District Court (St. Clair Shores)

27701 Jefferson Ave.

St. Clair Shores, MI 48081

(586) 445-5280

Honorable Mark A. Fratarcangeli, Chief Judge

Honorable Joseph Craigen Oster, District Judge

Ms. Carolyn A. Povich, Court Administrator

41A District Court (Sterling Heights)

40111 Dodge Park Rd.

Sterling Heights, MI 48313

(586) 446-2500

Honorable Stephen S. Sierawski, Chief Judge

Honorable Michael S. Maceroni, District Judge

Honorable Douglas P. Shepherd, District Judge

Honorable Kimberley Anne Wiegand, District Judge

Mr. Michael Piatek, Court Administrator

41A District Court (Shelby Township)

51660 Van Dyke Ave.

Shelby Township, MI 48316

(586) 739-7325

Honorable Stephen S. Sierawski, Chief Judge

Honorable Michael S. Maceroni, District Judge

Honorable Douglas P. Shepherd, District Judge

Honorable Kimberley Anne Wiegand, District Judge

Ms. Laura Porter, Court Administrator

41B District Court (Clinton Township)

22380 Starks Dr.

Clinton Township, MI 48036

(586) 469-9300

Honorable Carrie Lynn Fuca, Chief Judge

Honorable Linda Davis, District Judge

Honorable Sebastian Lucido, District Judge

42nd District Court (Romeo)

PO Box 6

14713 33 Mile Rd.

Romeo, MI 48065

(586) 752-9679

Honorable James M. Biernat, Jr., Chief Judge

Ms. Julie Bovenschen, Court Administrator

Honorable Denis R. LeDuc, District Judge

Ms. Sandy Kegler, Court Administrator

42nd District Court (New Baltimore)

35071 23 Mile Rd.

New Baltimore, MI 48047

(586) 725-9500

Honorable James M. Biernat, Jr., Chief Judge

Honorable William H. Hackel, III, District Judge

Ms. Marlisa Beauchemin, Court Administrator

WASHTENAW COUNTY

22nd Circuit Court

PO Box 8645

Courthouse

101 E. Huron

Ann Arbor, MI 48107

(734) 222-3270

Honorable David S. Swartz, Chief Judge

Honorable Archie Cameron Brown, Circuit Judge

Honorable Patrick J. Conlin, Jr., Circuit Judge

Honorable Timothy P. Connors, Circuit Judge

Honorable Carol Anne Kuhnke, Circuit Judge

14A-1 District Court (Pittsfield Township)

4133 Washtenaw Ave.

Ann Arbor, MI 48108

(734) 973-4545

Honorable Richard Conlin, District Judge

14A-2 District Court (Ypsilanti)

---

415 W. Michigan Ave.

Ypsilanti, MI 48197

(734) 484-6690

Honorable Kirk W. Tabbey, District Judge

Mr. Robert Ciolek, Court Administrator

14A-3 District Court (Chelsea)

---

122 S. Main St.

Chelsea, MI 48118

(734) 475-8606

Honorable Richard Conlin, District Judge

14A-4 District Court (Saline)

1000 N. Maple Rd.

Saline, MI, 48176

(734) 429-2504

Honorable Cedric J. Simpson, District Judge

14B District Court (Ypsilanti Township)

Ypsilanti Township Civic Center

7200 S. Huron River Drive

Ypsilanti, MI 48197

(734) 483-1333

Honorable Charles Pope, Chief Judge

Mr. Mark W. Nelson, Court Administrator

15th District Court (Ann Arbor)

PO Box 8650

Justice Center

301 E. Huron

Ann Arbor, MI 48104

(734) 794-6759

Honorable Joseph F. Burke, Chief Judge

Honorable Elizabeth Pollard Hines, District Judge

Honorable Karen Q. Valvo, District Judge

LAPEER COUNTY

40th Circuit Court

Lapeer County Complex

255 Clay Street

Lapeer, MI 48446

(810) 667-0320

Honorable Nick O. Holowka, Chief Judge

Honorable Byron J. Konschuh, Circuit Judge

Ms. Lori Curtiss, Court Administrator

Ms. Maureen Flanigan Salayko, Probate Register

Honorable Justus C. Scott, Probate Judge

71A District Court (Lapeer)

Lapeer County Complex Building

255 Clay Street

Lapeer, MI 48446

(810) 667-0314

Honorable Nick O. Holowka, Chief Judge

Honorable Laura Cheger Barnard, District Judge

Mr. Gregory K. Wise, Court Administrator

GENESEE COUNTY
7th Circuit Court

Genesee County Courthouse

900 S. Saginaw St.

Flint, MI 48502

(810) 424-4355

Honorable Richard B. Yuille, Chief Judge

Honorable Duncan M. Beagle, Circuit Judge

Honorable Joseph J. Farah, Circuit Judge

Honorable Judith A. Fullerton, Circuit Judge

Honorable John A. Gadola, Circuit Judge

Honorable Archie L. Hayman, Circuit Judge

Honorable Geoffrey L. Neithercut, Circuit Judge

Honorable David J. Newblatt, Circuit Judge

Honorable Michael J. Theile, Circuit Judge

Ms. Barbara A. Menear, Court Administrator

67th District Court (Flint)

---

630 S. Saginaw St.

Flint, MI 48502

(810) 257-3181

Honorable Richard B. Yuille, Chief Judge

Honorable David J. Goggins, District Judge

Mrs. Dena Altheide, Court Administrator

67th District Court (Burton)

4094 Manor Dr.

Burton, MI 48529

(810) 743-5600

Honorable Richard B. Yuille, Chief Judge

Honorable Mark W. Latchana, District Judge

Mrs. Dena Altheide, Court Administrator

67th District Court (Mt. Morris)

11820 N. Saginaw St.

Mt. Morris, MI 48458

(810) 686-7140

Honorable Richard B. Yuille, Chief Judge

Honorable Vikki Bayeh Haley, District Judge

Mrs. Dena Altheide, Court Administrator

67th District Court (Grand Blanc)

8173 S. Saginaw St.

Grand Blanc, MI 48439

(810) 694-2552

Honorable Richard B. Yuille, Chief Judge

Mrs. Dena Altheide, Court Administrator

67th District Court (Flint)

---

630 S. Saginaw St.

Flint, MI 48502

(810) 766-8968

Honorable Richard B. Yuille, Chief Judge

Honorable William H. Crawford, II, District Judge

Honorable G. David Guinn, District Judge

Mrs. Dena Altheide, Court Administrator

Honorable Herman Marable, Jr., District Judge

Honorable Nathaniel C. Perry, III, District Judge

LIVINGSTON COUNTY

44th Circuit Court

---

204 S. Highlander Way

Howell, MI 48843

(517) 546-8079

Honorable David Reader, Chief Judge

Honorable Michael P. Hatty, Circuit Judge

Mr. John H. Evans, Court Administrator

53rd District Court (Howell)

---

204 S. Highlander Way

Howell, MI 48843

(517) 548-1000

Honorable David Reader, Chief Judge

Honorable L. Suzanne Geddis, District Judge

Honorable Carol Sue Reader, District Judge

Ms. Francine Zysk, Court Administrator

53rd District Court (Brighton)

---

224 N 1st St,

Brighton, MI 48116

Howell, MI 48843

517-548-1000

Honorable Theresa Brennan, District Judge

KENT COUNTY

17th Circuit Court

Kent County Courthouse

180 Ottawa Ave., NW

Grand Rapids, MI 49503

(616) 632-5220

Honorable Donald A. Johnston, III, Chief Judge

Honorable Paul J. Denenfeld, Circuit Judge

Honorable Kathleen A. Feeney, Circuit Judge

Honorable Dennis B. Leiber, Circuit Judge

Honorable Deborah McNabb, Circuit Judge

Honorable George Jay Quist, Circuit Judge

Honorable J. Joseph Rossi, Circuit Judge

Honorable Paul J. Sullivan, Circuit Judge

Honorable Mark A. Trusock, Circuit Judge

Honorable Christopher P. Yates, Circuit Judge

Honorable Daniel V. Zemaitis, Circuit Judge

59th District Court (Grandville)

3161 Wilson Ave., S.W.

Grandville, MI 49418

(616) 538-9660

Honorable Peter P. Versluis, Chief Judge

Ms. Julie C. Fend, Court Administrator

59th District Court-Walker

4343 Remembrance Road N.W.

Walker, MI 49534

(616) 453-5765

Honorable Peter P. Versluis, Chief Judge

Ms. Julie C. Fend, Court Administrator

61st District Court (Kent)

Kent County Courthouse

180 Ottawa Ave., NW

Grand Rapids, MI 49503

(616) 632-5700

Honorable Jeanine Nemesi LaVille, Chief Judge

Honorable David J. Buter, District Judge

Honorable Michael J. Distel, District Judge

Honorable Christina Elmore, District Judge

Honorable Jennifer Faber, District Judge

Honorable Kimberly A. Schaefer, District Judge

Mr. Gary Paul Secor, Court Administrator

62A District Court (Wyoming)

Wyoming Justice Center 2650 DeHoop Ave.,

S.W.

Wyoming, MI 49509

(616) 530-7385

Honorable Steven M. Timmers, Chief Judge

Honorable Pablo Cortes, District Judge

Mr. Christopher Kittmann, Court Administrator

62B District Court (Kentwood)

4740 Walma Ave. SE

Kentwood, MI 49512

(616) 698-9310

Honorable William G. Kelly, Chief Judge

Ms. Michele White, Court Administrator

63rd District Court (Grand Rapids)

1950 E. Beltline Ave. NE

Grand Rapids, MI 49525

(616) 632-7770

Honorable Sara J. Smolenski, Chief Judge

Honorable Jeffrey J. O'Hara, District Judge

INGHAM COUNTY

30th Circuit Court

PO Box 40771

Veterans Memorial Courthouse

313 W. Kalamazoo St.

Lansing, MI 48901

(517) 483-6500

Honorable Janelle A. Lawless, Chief Judge

Honorable Rosemarie E. Aquilina, Circuit Judge

Honorable Laura Baird, Circuit Judge

Honorable Clinton Canady, III, Circuit Judge

Honorable Joyce Draganchuk, Circuit Judge

Honorable James S. Jamo, Circuit Judge

Ms. Shauna Dunnings, Court Administrator

54A District Court (Lansing)

City Hall, 6th Floor

124 W. Michigan Ave.

Lansing, MI 48933

(517) 483-4433

Honorable Louise Alderson, Chief Judge

Honorable Patrick F. Cherry, District Judge

Honorable Hugh B. Clarke, Jr., District Judge

Honorable Frank J. DeLuca, District Judge

Ms. Anethia O. Brewer, Court Administrator

54B District Court (East Lansing)
101 Linden St.

East Lansing, MI 48823

(517) 351-7000

Honorable Andrea Andrews Larkin, Chief Judge

Honorable Richard D. Ball, District Judge

Ms. Nicole Evans, Court Administrator

55th District Court (Mason)

700 Buhl Dr.

Mason, MI 48854

(517) 676-8400

Honorable Donald L. Allen, Chief Judge

Honorable Thomas P. Boyd, District Judge

Mr. Michael J. Dillon, Court Administrator

JACKSON COUNTY
4th Circuit Court

312 S. Jackson St.

Jackson, MI 49201

(517) 788-4268

Honorable Thomas D. Wilson, Chief Judge

Mr. Charles M. Adkins, Court Administrator

Honorable Susan Beebe Jordan, Circuit Judge

Honorable Richard N. LaFlamme, Circuit Judge

Honorable John G. McBain, Jr., Circuit Judge

12th District Court (Jackson)

Honorable Michael J. Klaeren, Chief Judge

Honorable Joseph S. Filip, District Judge

Honorable Daniel A. Goostrey, District Judge

Honorable R. Darryl Mazur, District Judge

Made in United States
Troutdale, OR
11/03/2026

56845404R00110